The Heart of Yoga Revealed

Judy L. White

Copyright © 2010 by Judy L. White, published by Truth Cross Publishing, PO Box 1488, Kingsland, Tx. 78639-9998, Library of Congress Cataloging-in-Publication Data

ISBN# 978-0-9843189-0-2
Printed in the USA

Cover Design by Jeremy Sartwell

Acknowledgements

This book would never have been written except that my LORD Jesus Christ laid it on my heart. Thank you, God, for giving me the desire and the grace to write this book and for surrounding me with gifted and talented friends and family to help along the way.

In particular, I would like to thank Debbie Sartwell for her dear friendship and undying faithfulness, for typing and editing year after year. I thank God for anointing Debbie for this work and giving her a steadfast heart. Without her, the manuscript would have no being.

In addition, I thank my cousin Jody Bosworth for helping me not only with initial plans and first drafts but also hours and hours of incredible editing through the years. Her gifts and extensive knowledge have been a God send in directing this effort and could not have been accomplished without her help.

Furthermore, I express heartfelt appreciation to my mother, Ethel Cosgrove, for her selfless love and assurance. I love and thank her for being a wonderful role model. She is such an important influence in my life.

And to my sister, Deborah Graham, I am grateful for thorough research and exhaustive efforts to apprehend sources for this book. I thank her for constant edification and advice when we at length discussed excerpts from the "rough drafts."

I also want to thank my friend, Elizabeth Winter, for being attentive to God by her willingness to share her testimony, which I have recorded in this book. I am blessed by her input and tedious confirmation of each Scripture.

Also, I want to thank Donna McCreary for her heartfelt and incredibly detailed Holy Spirit led input and notes, Gloria Harvell, for her extremely creative insight and loving critique.

A special thanks to my very blessed children and their spouses, Erich, Jill, Jennifer, Tim, Dustin and Crystal for their loving support and patience through the years in this endeavor.

Most of all, I am thankful for my husband, Rickey, for whom I have an endless and undying love. It was his constant encouragement, generous support, and unselfish love that afforded me the means to persist in my mission. It is an honor to be the wife of such a man.

Introduction

This book reveals the occult language of the yoga vocabulary. Hidden within the ancient postures is a sign language containing the Sanskrit (Indian) alphabet. These letters make up mantras (power words) when illuminated by the Kundalini (serpent power). The mantras automatically transmit vibrations evoking the ancient Hindu gods. These Hindu gods are revealed as Satan's angels of darkness.

Yoga's ancient religious ritual is Satan's scheme, hidden for ages and covered by elaborate design. Ancient holy sacred writings prove yoga's origin to be solely for religious purposes in order to consummate a union with their Hindu gods.

As a Christian, you must understand the adversary. You are God's chosen child. You are called by His name. You are not Satan's pawn. Do not live your life as though you are posturing yourself upon the chessboard of compromise!

The Heart of Yoga Revealed! invites you to explore how the LORD Jesus Christ by His Holy Spirit reveals the truth about the incredible facade of the yoga phenomenon.

Table of Contents

Table of Contents

Chapter

Yoga
Union with the "Universal World Soul"

Yoga is a commonplace word that fifty years ago was rarely known to western civilization. When a person hears the word yoga, they view it as an exercise and immediately envision a person on a mat doing poses and stretches to help the body and mind. It is seen on commercials, TV shows, and even the health professionals tout the benefits of yoga but how does yoga supposedly benefit the mind and body?

Does it have a double-edged sword permeating the mind and body with negative side effects? Does the Christian need to be concerned about such negative side effects? How do yogi masters define yoga? Who created yoga and why was it created? The purpose throughout this book is to reveal the double-edged sword of yoga and its ramifications experienced by the practitioner. Exactly what is the definition of yoga?

According to *Webster's New World Dictionary, Third College Edition's* primary definition, yoga is purely a religious discipline of the Hindu faith:

> 1. a mystic and ascetic Hindu discipline by which one seeks to achieve liberation of the self and union with the supreme spirit or universal soul through intense concentration, deep meditation, and practices involving prescribed postures, controlled breathing, etc.

The *Encarta World English Dictionary's* primary definition of yoga is also based on religion:

> Yoga: Hindu discipline, any of a group of related Hindu disciplines that promote the unity of the individual with a supreme being through a system of postures and rituals. *NOT JEHOVAH !!*

Those who practice yoga as a system of physical exercise and breathing control are actually practicing an ancient system designed to elicit mystical experiences and occult spiritual insights.

Many people are under the false impression that yoga's primary objective is to bring unity to their spirit, soul, and body. Yet, nothing could be further from the truth. Yoga's primary objective is to bring their spirit, soul, and body into unity with Hindu gods.

Random House Webster's College Dictionary's secondary definition emphasizes spiritual unity:

> Yoga: A school of Hindu philosophy using such a system to unify the Self with the Supreme Being or ultimate principle.

Yoga's religious rituals demonstrating the Hindu scriptures date back thousands of years. The earliest references to yoga come from carvings dating back as far as 2800 B.C.E. that were found in the Indus Valley (in modern Pakistan). The Vedas (scriptures) come from a Sanskrit speaking race which are different laws given by the Lord (Krishna). There is a huge varied collection of texts among which are the upanishads (meaning to sit down next to a guru in order to learn) and the "*Bhagavad-Gita* is the science of Krsna [Krishna] consciousness" (*Bhagavad-Gita As It Is*, pg. 106).

Yoga enters the world through Hindu gods

The *Bhagavad-Gita* claims to be the essence of India's Vedic wisdom and one of the great spiritual and philosophical classics of the world. According to the *Bhagavad-Gita*, yoga came to our world passed down through a series of Hindu gods:

> The Blessed Lord [Krishna] first instructed this imperishable science of *yoga* to the sun-god, Vivansvān. Vivansvān instructed it to Manu, the father of mankind, and Manu in turn instructed it to Iksviku (his son). (*Bhagavad-Gita As It Is*, plate 16, pg. 63)

The *Bhagavad-Gita As It Is*, the definitive and holy sacred text of Hindu doctrine recorded by ancient ascended masters, defines yoga as "linking with the Supreme," which is Brahman (pg. 283).

Unfortunately, most Christians do not understand that by its own definition, yoga is an occult religious ritual practiced through *postures, mudras* (occult hand signals), and *mantras* (chanted incantations) which are themselves ancient magical incantations. These religious rituals are implanted within yoga practice and dedicated to seeking union with Hindu gods.

Furthermore, Christians do not realize that yoga's breathing techniques are dangerous and <u>subliminally alter</u> ✻ <u>levels of consciousness</u>. Many Christians do not recognize that yoga's ultimate aim is to create a union with a "divine force," also known as "a supreme spirit," or what Hindu yogi masters term "oneness with the Universal Soul."

Even hand signs, called *mudras,* are a language which signal worship to Hindu mystic gods through an ancient alphabet. This *sign language* is understood in the spirit realm as <u>admiration and submissive sacrifice</u>.

When the yoga instructor leads the practitioner into the lotus position or Buddha posture, the fingers gesture the eastern mystical religious symbols of the yin and the yang. These polarized opposites, goddess and god, female and male, represent union of the forces.

Yoga is, by definition, the act of yoking the practitioner to Brahman, the "Divine" higher self, who is said to enlighten the soul. According to the Hindu text, enlightenment of mankind comes from union with Brahman. Brahman not only brings enlightenment, he also claims to be the "Universal World Soul." Through intense concentration, controlled breathing techniques, and prescribed yoga postures, Brahman and yoga practitioners are united as one.

Yoga is further explained by imagining it as a tree:

> It has big, tangled roots, a gigantic stem, several huge branches, numerous secondary branches, and countless twigs. Some of the branches are

quite dead, while others are very much alive, blossoming anew every spring. (*Living Yoga*, pg. 8)

These huge branches are yoga's eight "limbs" which keep the physical exercises connected to its spiritual roots:

Each "limb" has a spiritual goal and together they form a unit .... Because the eight steps are interdependent, the steps of 'postures' and 'breathing' cannot logically be separated from the others. Thus, the interdependence of all eight steps reveals why the physical exercises of Yoga are *designed* to prepare the body for the spiritual (occult) changes that will allegedly help one realize godhood status. (*Encyclopedia of New Age Beliefs*, pg. 601)

Before we eat the fruit of the yoga tree, we need to look at the origin and nature of its seed. The Bible explains this concept:

Then God said, "Let the earth bring forth grass, the herb that yields seed, and the fruit tree that yields fruit according to its kind, whose seed is in itself, on the earth"; and it was so. (Genesis 1:11, NKJ)

...if the root is holy, so are the branches. (Romans 11:16b, NKJ)

For a good tree does not bear bad fruit, nor does a bad tree bear good fruit. (Luke 6:43, NKJ)

Does a spring send forth fresh water and bitter
from the same opening? Can a fig tree, my
brethren, bear olives, or a grapevine bear figs?
Thus no spring yields both salt water and fresh.
(James 3:11-12, NKJ)

These verses explain that we cannot separate the nature
of the seed from the nature of the tree, nor can we separate
the nature of the branches from the nature of the fruit. The
fruit is either good or evil depending on the nature of the seed.

The seed of yoga produces a religious practice that serves
and worships false gods. The nature of the yoga seed is
evil, and anything that is evil is enmity with God (Gen.
3:15). Yoga's evil seed produces fruits of idol worship, self-
glorification, and the sin of pride, all the attributes of Satan.

The ancient history of yoga is steeped in occult Taoism,
Hinduism, and Zen Buddhism, which are the mystical
forerunners of current New Age doctrine. These false religions
embrace the great lie of Satan, which is that we should exalt
self -will over God's will. This rebellious practice began with
Adam and Eve in the garden.

In practicing yoga, Satan manipulates the function of
breathing. Our breath is our first gift from God. Who would
think that the act of breathing could be altered to exalt self?

Hatha yoga – Primary limb of yoga

When you practice yoga, you are manipulating God's
first gift by seductively mastering and controlling the breath.
Satan perpetuated his plan of bewitchment ages ago with

the inception of hatha yoga. Hatha yoga means *"union with the breath."* *The Shambhala Encyclopedia of Yoga* reveals that the "breath ritual . . . is the sacrifice of one's breath into the Divine" (pg. 181).

Hatha yoga, the primary limb of the yoga tree, is considered by many to be harmless and one of the most common of all the branches. Yet it is far from harmless because it holds the power to alter your mind. The connection between breathing and altered states of consciousness is explained in the *Encyclopedia of New Age Beliefs*:

> If one considers the ancient yoga science of pranayama (controlled breathing) to have relevance, then one must admit that the manual manipulation of the nasal cycle during meditation (dhyana) is the most thoroughly documented of techniques for altering consciousness.

> [T]his nasal cycle [is linked] to the ancient yogic traditions of *pranayama* (breath control) in achieving psychosomatic health and the transpersonal states of *dhyana* (deep concentration) and *samadhi* (occult enlightenment). (pg. 596)

"Occult enlightenment" is a term that is at the heart of the purpose of yoga. The definition of "occult" according to *Webster's New World Dictionary* is something that is concealed:

> 1. hidden; concealed. 2. secret; esoteric.
> 3. beyond human understanding; mysterious.
> 4. designating or of certain alleged mystic arts, magic, alchemy, astrology, etc.

Within the definition for "occult," the word "esoteric" is used. Esoteric is a term that implies a deep, hidden perspective. The word "esoteric" refers to a secretive inner circle of conveyed knowledge or Gnostic wisdom given to a select few.

Gnosticism is an occult salvation system, a system that embraces a conglomeration of unorthodox religious beliefs. Yoga practice is an esoteric system, which touts itself to possess superior spiritual knowledge, gained by self-illumination and limited to an elite few.

Therefore, yoga can be defined as a practice of occult knowledge, magic, or witchcraft. The implication of the definition leads us to assume that by practicing these black arts, we can uncover mysteries. One mystery we must uncover, the yoga gurus tell us, is the "revelation" of the knowledge that we are "One" with the cosmic forces of the universe.

Yoga reveals mysteries of godhood?

According to these ancient and modern yoga gurus, when we accept who we are in terms of the universe, then we become enlightened to all the mysteries of godhood. Along with other occult means, enlightenment comes through practicing hatha yoga, which employs breath control. Through breath control, the yoga practitioner becomes "One" with the godhead, the universal life force.

By contrast, Christian believers accept who we are in Jesus Christ and understand that by grace we become One with God through faith in Him (Ephesians 2:8). Deep breathing may help oxygenate our bodies, give us expanded lung capacity, a giddy sense of light-headedness, a dangerous brush with a moment of hyperventilation, or even an altered state of reality, but it will not, nor will it ever, bring us into oneness with the Living God.

But according to swamis, hatha yoga is the key to power and control of the natural and cosmic world, and controlling the breath will enable you to become God. The breath (prana) is the key to the universe and all that is within it. Prana is believed to be universal divine energy.

Swami Nikhilananada describes this energy as "the infinite, omnipresent manifesting power of this universe. Perfect control of prana makes one God. One can have infinite knowledge, infinite power, now" (*Encyclopedia of New Age Beliefs,* pg. 601).

Do you see how the eastern mystics imitate, just as Satan does, the attributes of God? God's breath is the beginning of life. "And the LORD God formed man of the dust of the ground, and breathed into his nostrils the breath of life; and man became a living being" (Genesis 2:7).

Manipulations of the breath

God's created human being is perfect and wonderful, made to breathe deeply on his own without esoteric manipulations. Using breathing repetition to stimulate and apprehend the subconscious perverts God's gift of breath to our detriment and has in many cases, become the cause of mental illness and death.

A newspaper article reports what takes place naturally in our bodies when we take deep breaths a couple of times throughout the day, but then the article exalts yoga as a discipline to enhance the breathing. Doctors Mike Roizen and Mehmet Oz explain the process:

> All you need to do is breathe. Inhaling deeply brings a chemical called nitric oxide from the back of your nose and your sinuses into your lungs. This short-lived gas dilates the air passages in your lungs and does the same to the blood vessels surrounding them so you can get oxygen into your body. Nitric oxide also doubles as a neurotransmitter to help your brain function.... Yoga is an excellent way to train yourself to take these deep breaths. A yoga sequence or two in the morning helps you get your blood going.... (Ft. Worth Texas Star Telegram Newspaper, March 30, 2009, pg. 8a)

We all need to breathe deeply in order to bring oxygen into our bodies but we do not need the disciplines of yoga to accomplish this task. Too much deep breathing, which yoga promotes, can have toxic effects on the body:

> The overproduction of nitric oxide in brain tissues has been implicated in stroke and other neurological problems...[i.e.] Huntington's disease and Alzheimer's disease.... During a massive bacterial infection, excess nitric oxide can go into the vascular system, causing a dramatic decrease in blood pressure, which may lead to possible fatal septic shock. (www.absw.org.uk/briefings/nitric%20oxide.htm)

Natural deep breathing is good for the immune system and serves as a crucial biological function but the focus on intense breathing can be toxic:

> ...too much nitric oxide is extremely toxic and will cause death of nerve cells; so within the kernel of this important signaling mechanism are the potential seeds for neuro-degeneration, which if left unchecked contribute to the pathologies of stroke and dementias. (www.brainmysteries.com)

A little known fact is that virtually every major guru in India has issued warnings that describe the ill-effects of _undisciplined_ yoga practice. But these same gurus exalt the _disciplined_ practice of yoga. They teach that a union with Brahman (the Universal World Soul) is the goal of the yogi. _The Complete Yoga Book_ defines this union as an absorption into metaphysical oneness:

> Yoga is Indian and Hindu; and for the Hindu mystic the supreme goal in living is absorption in Brahman.... In the purest Yoga, which is that of the _upanishads_ (Hindu scriptures), Brahman is impersonal and imageless... (_The Complete Yoga Book_, pg. 3)

Should Christians practice a discipline that seeks to unite its practitioners with occultism? A union with idols would spiritually adulterate our relationship with Jesus. Only by the blood of Christ, the Lamb of God, will we become one with God the Father. Jesus understood that He and His Father were one, and He prayed for us to become one with them.

"...that they all may be one, as You, Father, are in Me, and I in You; that they also may be one in Us, that the world may believe that You sent Me." (John 17:21, NKJ)

God's promise of *oneness* has been imitated by all occult religions whose author is Satan. The path to achieving *oneness* within these false religions is far different from the Christian path. Christians cannot earn their salvation through deeds and rituals, yet certain practices, works, and disciplines are the very means by which occult religious leaders believe they earn their *oneness* with divinity.

Yoga masters teach that humans have merely forgotten their union with divinity and that certain acts will bring forth remembrance:

> The esoteric tradition tells us that we come from (or are grounded in) the One Self, that we are estranged from or unaware of our origin, and that we can return not through learning, but by remembering our true identity. (*Living Yoga*, pg. 151)

The notion that *oneness* with God may be achieved within the discipline of yoga, the practice of Buddhism, or the worship of Hindu gods implies that there are many ways to reach divine status. This false doctrine perjures the truth of the Bible, it denies that Jesus Christ has a holy union with the Father, and it disputes that He is in covenant with those who are cleansed by His blood.

Yoga beliefs reject the truth that Jesus Christ is the one and only way to God the Father, but the Bible is indelibly clear:

> ...how much more shall the blood of Christ, who through the eternal Spirit offered Himself without spot to God, cleanse your conscience from dead works to serve the living God? And for this reason He is the Mediator of the new covenant by means of death, for the redemption of the transgressions under the first covenant, that those who are called may receive the promise of the eternal inheritance. (Heb. 9:14-15, NKJ)

Eastern mystical religions dilute the blood sacrifice of Jesus Christ and deny His resurrection power. They claim that Brahma, Siva, Vishnu, Confucius, Buddha, Mohammed, Allah, and Krishna along with their many other gods and false prophets are equal to Jesus Christ and possess the ability to bring salvation to mankind.

Jesus Christ, the Creator of all things (John 1:3) makes known to us the only way to salvation:

> "I am the way, the truth, and the life. No one comes to the Father except through Me."
> (John 14:6, NKJ)

> For God did not appoint us to wrath, but to obtain salvation through our LORD Jesus Christ, who died for us, that whether we wake or sleep, we should live together with Him.
> (I Thess. 5:9 -10, NKJ)

Who are Brahma, Siva, Vishnu, Confucius, Buddha, Mohammed, Allah, and Krishna? Are they truly coequal with Jesus Christ, God's only begotten son? Do they possess the Divinity of God, the Almighty Father, the God of Abraham, Isaac, and Jacob? The truth is found in the words of ancient biblical prophets. Malachi, Jeremiah, and Isaiah proclaim the knowledge of the One True and Living God.

> Have we not all one Father? Has not one God created us? Why do we deal treacherously with one another by profaning the covenant of the fathers? (Malachi 2:10, NKJ)

> But the LORD is the true God; He is the living God and the Everlasting King. (Jeremiah 10:10a, NKJ)

> "Look to Me, and be saved, all you ends of the earth! For I am God, and there is no other." (Isaiah 45:22, NKJ)

> "...I am God, and there is none else." (Isaiah 45:22b, King James)

There are three basic claims among occult religions that blatantly deny the Gospel. These claims are that human beings are potential gods, all living things are part of the same common unit, and each individual may be absolved of sin by reincarnation or personal religious performance.

Embraced by the eastern mystic and now by the western yogi is the notion that God is found in many forms, as many forms as there are individuals who give them credibility. Even more accepted is the distorted concept that mankind has no need for redemption, salvation, or remission of sin. The individual self is able to be transformed into an enlightened god and become its own agent for reaching divinity.

> Now all those wild little desires can be acted out without real risk because it is God playing the game with himself. The Hindu term for this is Maha-lila [great play, sport]. One can sin without consequence since it is all a cosmic game of hide-and-seek anyway. (*One World*, pg. 214)

The Hindu holy book expresses the same ethic:

> ...[M]any westerners use the guru's argument from the *Bhagavad-Gita*: that any action is permissible if done in the right consciousness, even killing. (pg. 214)

This doctrine of Maha-lila is similar to the warped logic used by Osama Bin Ladin and his militant, suicidal followers. Radical Muslims sincerely believe that if they kill infidels, specifically Christians and Jews, Allah will be pleased, and then they earn a martyr's reward, which is instant acceptance into heaven. Of course we know that murder is a sin and that hate permeates the heart of Satan. He only comes to steal, kill, and destroy (John 10:10). Clearly his target is the image of God in the earth, God's people. Satan has a plot but God has a plan:

> ...without shedding of blood there is no remission [of sin]. (Heb. 9:22b, NKJ)

...He has appeared to put away sin by the sacrifice of Himself. (Heb. 9:26b, NKJ)

...so Christ was offered once to bear the sins of many. (Heb. 9:28a, NKJ)

"...through His name, whoever believes in Him will receive remission of sins." (Acts 10:43, NKJ)

The New Testament makes it clear that sin does not absolve itself and that our salvation comes only through Jesus Christ. Yet, according to eastern philosophy, salvation comes by way of cosmic consciousness. The Atman or pure cosmic consciousness is the source of salvation and is found only through yoga.

The Complete Yoga Book explains the connection of yoga to the cosmos:

> In the West today, a psychological orientation makes Being, Self beyond empirical ego, and levels of consciousness the terms in which the loftiest aims of Yoga are most meaningfully discussed.
>
> The Self to be realized beyond the ego in Indian Yoga is the *Atman*. Find the *Atman*, which is pure consciousness, through Yogic practice, and you find (the intuitive enlightenment called *samadhi*) that individual being and Cosmic Being have the same ground, and that *Atman* and *Brahman* are one. (pg. 3)

Hindu world view sold to westerners

Several yoga masters and esoteric teachers openly admit the religious and spiritual aspects of yoga. They know that yoga is far more than an exercise for physical fitness. They boast that the west is "open-minded" and eager to become involved with the trendy search for divine self. They readily expose their motives as they explain how yoga is being packaged and sold to the west:

> If a person says he is interested in yoga simply as a physical discipline, he should be told that it was not invented by the mystic masters of old simply to cultivate better physiques. Yoga teachers such as R.L. Hittleman admit that any health benefits are secondary. He also admits to having used the health angle to hook Westerners on the Hindu worldview. (*Confronting the New Age*, pg. 79)

The "mystic masters of old" knew that an empty mind is the most receptive. In essence, yogic philosophy teaches, "Not to know is the beginning of knowledge." The yogi is taught to empty his mind so that the eastern philosophy may be easily received. In contrast to yogic open-mindedness, Christians are to fill their minds with the Word of God in order to gain His wisdom, knowledge, and understanding.

> "The fear of the Lord is the beginning of wisdom, and the knowledge of the Holy One is understanding." (Prov. 9:10, NKJ)

> All Scripture is given by inspiration of God, and is profitable for doctrine, for reproof, for

correction, for instruction in righteousness, that the man of God may be complete, thoroughly equipped for every good work. (II Tim. 3:16, 17, NKJ)

We are commanded to guard our minds with the knowledge of Jesus Christ.

Therefore gird up the loins of your mind... (I Peter 1:13a, NKJ)

Unfortunately, unsuspecting yoga practitioners who are void of the Word of God leave themselves wide open for spiritual deception masquerading as "intuitive knowledge." This occult knowledge is manifested as energy flashes and travels through seven chakras, located in the supple body, called the "psychic centers."

One of the highest of these seven energy centers, located in the middle of the forehead, also known as the Third Eye, is called the Ajna Chakra:

Ajna is the witnessing centre where one becomes the detached observer of all events, including those within the body and mind. Here the level of awareness is developed whereby one begins to "see" the hidden essence underlying all visible appearances. When Ajna (the Third Eye) is awakened, the meaning and significance of symbols flashes into one's conscious perception and intuitive knowledge arises effortlessly.... up until Ajna chakra awakens, we are under delusion. It is only after awakening of Ajna

Chakra (the Third Eye) that the laws of cause and effect can be known. (www.adishakti. org/miscellaneous/battle_of_armageddon) 2/13/2003

"Oh to be as gods," say the yoga masters. To know what God knows has been the desire of man since his creation.

If we persist in practicing yoga, the process of awakening the "Third Eye" to the voices of the hidden mysteries of the occult is the catalyst that will ultimately bring us into agreement with the Adversary of God. Our brainwashed minds (souls) are then so defiled with such clamoring that God's voice is not heard. Unable to hear from God, we may begin to seek other avenues of "knowledge" such as psychic readings or our horoscopes. But be assured that any "Third Eye" spiritual intuition received by occult means does not come from the One True God.

If we are having trouble recognizing false religions, then we must simply trust God's Word. God warns us not to practice other religious rituals even if they seem good in our eyes. He speaks of deadly results for those who insist on having their own way and who have their own ideas of good and evil, right and wrong. He clearly tells us what to do:

> "Be sure to obey all my instructions. And remember, never pray to or swear by any other gods. Do not even mention their names.... Do not worship the gods of these other nations or serve them in any way, and never follow their evil example. Instead, you must utterly conquer them and break down their shameful idols....

Make no treaties with them and have nothing to do with their gods. Do not even let them live among you! If you do, they will infect you with the sin of idol worship, and that would be disastrous for you." (Exodus 23:13, 24, 32-33, New Living Translation)

The Gentile nations, specific to Exodus 23, consisted of the Hittites, Perizzites, Amorites, and Canaanites and were the enemies of God's Hebrew children. God's Word is still to this day applicable to anyone who worships false gods, including mythological deities, totems, animals, birds, statues, stones, dead ancestors, spirit guides, and cosmic or astrological forces.

Hinduism has a triune god

Let's take a look at one of these cosmic forces so that we may better understand the foundation of the religious practice of yoga. Let's examine the structural basis of the gods of the Hindu religion. Those who profess Hinduism have a triune god of their own, a deity called Brahma, Vishnu, and Siva. All are manifested into one whom they call Brahman, or the Universal Soul.

Hindus perceive this triune force in terms of universal cosmic energy which generates a male supernatural spiritual presence. In the Chinese culture, the male essence is termed "yang," opposite of "yin," which is female. Hindus believe that humans are "yin," the earthly counterpart to their triune male god. When the two are "yogied" or united together, they are made "one."

Through this "yogied oneness," Hindus believe humans will be "enlightened" to eternal salvation as they become "one" with Brahman. The Christian knows there is only one way to salvation. In the book of Romans, Paul courageously proclaims that only the Gospel of Jesus Christ brings salvation, and that salvation is offered to Jews and Greeks, meaning all mankind:

> For I am not ashamed of the gospel of Christ, for it is the power of God to salvation for everyone who believes, for the Jew first and also for the Greek. (Romans 1:16, NKJ)

Since the beginning of time there has been a yearning among all humans to be connected to divinity within a supernatural world. Our spirits and souls (minds, wills, and emotions) are like vacuums waiting to be filled. The great apostasy among mankind is that we have failed to fill that vacuum with God and His Word.

Brahman does indeed inhabit the supernatural world, but he does not love us. Neither does the cosmos love us. How foolish of us as Christians to pursue a connection with an idol god or an aspect of creation that exists in rebellion to Almighty God, rather than to desire to be yoked with the Creator Himself.

When you practice yoga, you bow to idols. In yoga, Brahman is the "Divine" in each of us. Namaste is the gesture of bowing to the "Divine" in each other. "Namaste literally means 'bow me you' [Brahman] or 'I bow to you' [Brahman]" (www.yogajournal.com/basics/822).

Brahman is not the God of Abraham, Isaac and Jacob. Brahman is not even a personal god to the Hindu. In the Hindu pantheon, Brahman is simply cosmic energy. He is called the "Divine higher-self" or Universal World Soul. Brahman is not to be confused with Brahma, the first god of the Hindu trinity who oversees a pantheon of 330 million other Hindu gods.

Many within the Hindu faith believe that these millions of gods are likened to angels. Hindus pray to them for different needs. To one they pray for financial prosperity, to another for good luck, and to another for healing.

Clearly this Hindu belief is in rebellion to God's Word. Christians are instructed in the Bible NOT to bow to or pray to angels. Christians pray only to God the Father, in the name of Jesus Christ the Son, by the power of the Holy Spirit. Through our submission to Him, we trust that our Father God will indeed send His blessings, meet all of our needs according to His riches in glory, and when we delight ourselves in the LORD, He will fulfill our heart's desires (Ephesians 3:16 and Psalm 37:4).

Holy angels and fallen angels

Angels are created heavenly beings that exist to carry out the will of God. We are instructed by God not to worship angels, not to serve or bow down to them or to anything that is in heaven above or beneath the earth (Exodus 20:3-5).

God's angels certainly have their place in our lives. God ordains them to minister on our behalf. Because of His great love for us, God sends His ministering spirits to keep us from harm:

> For He shall give His angels charge over you, to keep you in all your ways. In their hands they shall bear you up, lest you dash your foot against a stone. (Psalm 91:11-12, NKJ)

We know, through God's Word, that there are holy angels and renegade angels. The renegade angels are demonic fallen angels, followers of Satan. God's holy angels are servants of Jesus Christ on mankind's behalf.

In the following Scripture, we see that John was given revelation through one of God's holy angels. John records the conversation:

> Then he [the angel] said to me, "Write, 'Blessed are those who are called to the marriage supper of the Lamb!'" And he said to me, "These are the true sayings of God." And I fell at his feet to worship him. But he said to me, "See that you do not do that! I am your fellow servant, and of your brethren who have the testimony of Jesus." (Revelation 19:9-10a, NKJ).

Clearly, the angel of the LORD commanded John not to bow down or worship him. The God of the Bible forbids the worship of or union with angels. Uniting with and being possessed by Satan's angels will always bring mankind into bondage.

Yet, after a session of yoga posturing, meditation, and bowing, yoga players have made contact with Satan's angels. The yoga adept emerges from their yoga mat "enlightened" with the belief that they have been imparted with esoteric wisdom from the "Divine" cosmic universe.

Deceived by Satan's angels, yoga practitioners are convinced that they have encountered the enlightened Kingdom of God. However, in reality, men and women on their yoga mats unknowingly connect themselves to the demonic supernatural realm. As they perform ancient magical postures, altering subconscious breath controls and incantations, they have encountered Satan's kingdom of darkness known as the "Universal World Soul," Brahman.

Chapter 2

East Meets West
Yoga Comes to America

Yoga in America is a fairly new phenomenon. It has taken literally thousands of years for it to find its way into our still young culture. How did the eastern mystical mindset find a foothold in America?

Immigrants from the Middle East migrated during the 1960's and are still arriving to this day. They came to find freedom to raise families and to establish businesses in lucrative U.S. markets. They brought their culture and their religions with them. It is a fact that yoga migrated to the west first as a spiritual discipline. This occurred at the time when "free love," vegetarianism, and non-violence were promoted quite effectively as key elements of yogic philosophy.

As the western media began its love affair with foreign cultures, American consumers were introduced to new ideas about religion, relationships, and relativity. Gradually, predominately western ideas of absolute values were questioned and replaced with eastern concepts of relativism. The foreign notion of good and evil as equal and co-existing in relative cosmic tension gave birth to a cultural revolution. This idea was welcomed in the classroom, where *situational ethics* taught that wrong is wrong only in certain situations.

The itching ears of the consuming American media were tickled with the merging of marketplace values, intellectualism, religion and eastern culture. In their frenzy for revolutionary ideas, networks and media publishers covered such events as the meeting between George Harrison, from the "Beatles," and his spiritual guru from India.

Furthermore, when the Dalai Lama chose to visit our shores to spread his "wisdom," American celebrities began to champion his cause, becoming Buddhists in the wake. Caught up in the adoration of celebrities, the public took notice of the religious movement of movie stars.

Eventually, coupled with the influence of eastern religions, the changing culture began its long experimentation with prolific drug use and ushered in the mesmerizing idea of the *altered consciousness*. As the celebration of altered consciousness came into vogue and the elements of pop culture (TV, movies, music, and fitness) intertwined with the forces of academia, religion, and commerce, America underwent a paradigm shift and began its easternized transformation.

Ancient religions newly revived, along with their gods, found a happy home in the altered consciousness of westerners. The Fifth Dimension's *"Age of Aquarius"* sprang from pop to mainstream culture, and George Harrison's *"My Sweet Lord"* blended the identity of Jesus and Krishna. A New Age of spiritual enlightenment dawned, and the east and west blended through yoga's New Age dialogue.

The unguarded church

Yoga penetrated the fortress walls of the unguarded church. A good analogy of the invasion of yoga within the Kingdom of God is the legend of the Trojan horse:

> ... [A] huge, hollow wooden horse with Greek soldiers hidden inside that is left at the gates of Troy: when the Trojans bring it into the city, the soldiers creep out and open the gates to the rest of the Greek army, which destroys the city. (*Webster's Family Encyclopedia*)

Likewise, yoga is offered at the gates of the Church. When the Christians bring it into the Kingdom of God, the soldiers of Satan creep out and open the unguarded gates to the rest of the demons, which destroys the unguarded church. Satan is continually seeking whom he may devour (I Peter 5:8). It is the unguarded churches that are being invaded and devoured. They are lacking the fear of the LORD which is the beginning of wisdom (Prov. 9:10), not living to serve God but only themselves.

Another example of a "wolf in sheep's clothing" is that of Adolf Hitler's diabolical snare to enslave and murder the Jews. He practiced many of the black arts of eastern mysticism yet professed to be a Christian in order to seduce and motivate his army to pursue his covert operations against God's people. Hitler lied and sold the Darwinian notion of the innate superiority of the Arian race and blamed the Jews for Germany's defeat in World War I. Hitler was able to implement policies of unparalleled atrocities going unchecked for over a decade.

How did yoga and Hitler seduce God's people? Satan perverts God's Word. He invades the Kingdom of God through the guise of righteousness. He makes it look good and presents his evil ideas as wise and personally favorable.

Desensitizing Christians to other religions

The dimming of the Light of God's Word and the merging, or blurring, of distinctions between east and west is a goal of the New Age Religion. We are evolving, New Agers claim with joy, into a New World Order with one world government, one world economy, and one world religion.

For spiritual New Agers who welcome the New World Order, the art of esoteric yoga is a valuable asset and perfectly suits their purposes. They believe that yoga will perform its task of desensitizing Christians to other forms of religious beliefs. In the practice of yoga, unaware Christians become incrementally transformed into mechanical followers of eastern mysticism and New Age philosophy.

In the lives of many Christians, the methodology of transformation has already worked its magic. Cultural change has occurred without particular notice, and certainly without our objection. In various mystic circles, the yoga spirit congratulates itself for our unconscious, or subconscious, acceptance of its intrusion upon our lives and into our culture. We have allowed the spirit of yoga to live within our American institutions as if this religious ritual came to our shores on the Mayflower with the Pilgrims.

The connections between pagan rites, eastern mysticism, yoga, and the New Age movement are not easily discernible to the average consumer of religion and culture, but the connection is strong and viable. Hinduism, Buddhism, the New Age religion, and other religious practices are finally united in a polygamous marriage. Yoga is their common husband and the New Age is their offspring, keeping the spirit of the New Age yoga religion alive and thriving.

The 2008 statistics on yoga reveal "15.8 million Americans practice yoga. Americans spend 5.7 billion dollars a year on yoga classes and products" (www.yogajournal.com/advertise/pressrelease/10). We know that yoga has entered the mainstream when anyone can buy yoga equipment at the nearest department store or pick up books like *Yoga for Dummies* or *The Complete Idiot's Guide to Yoga with Kids*. Many TV shows and movies show actors and actresses in various postures and tout yoga to be beneficial.

> Peter Jones in his Christian Witness to a Pagan Planet e-newsletter reports that twenty million Americans practice yoga including Madonna, Oprah, Gwyneth Paltrow, Monica Lewinski, Hillary Clinton, Phil Jackson (with many L.A. Lakers) the Gores and Sandra Day O'Connor, of the Supreme Court. (www.letusreason.org pg. 2 4-1-2009)

Doing yoga changes you spiritually?

Most people defend yoga believing that they have become more "spiritual" since they began practicing yoga.

Many do not consider themselves to be serving actively in any particular religion nor do they claim to be avid followers of Jesus Christ, yet they boast "spirituality."

An article in the Fort Worth (Texas) Star-Telegram Newspaper concurs with what many have already said about the "spiritual" phenomenon coinciding with the practice of yoga. Stacy Stier, co-owner of Bikram Yoga in Grapevine, Texas, says, "The spiritual aspects of yoga come to those who practice it whether or not they seek them.... The spiritual part just occurs, whether you are looking for it or not.... It's the silence, it's the time to be with your breath.... You learn to be open, flexible and at peace" (Oct. 21, 2002 Pg 7D).

Even yoga master and author of *The Heart of Yoga* T. K. V. Desikachar cannot explain this spiritual phenomenon.

> We do well to respect the fact that, to some people, the concept of Iśvara [Universal World Soul] means nothing at all.... I don't know how it happens, but in the course of time [spent doing yoga] their attitude toward the concept of Iśvara almost always changes. A kind of respect develops, and gradually they begin to accept the existence of something that is higher than we are.... This happens with people of very different backgrounds, and this change almost always occurs. (pg. 129)

Both Stier and Desikachar admit these changes occur without the practitioner's conscious effort regardless of their knowledge, desire, or permission. An unseen force affects them and changes their spiritual world view simply by performing yoga postures.

For the lack of a better description of this occurrence, yoga gurus choose to gloss over the phenomenon by calling it "spiritual" as if somehow that makes it less religious in nature. However, in reality this demonic spiritual phenomenon should be considered an invasion of the soul (mind, will, and emotions). But the yogis and the New Age movement embrace this invasion as a kind of mystical encounter.

The devil is no respecter of persons!

In fact, one expert in demonology, Kent Philpott, refers to the dangers of occultism:

> Probably the most dangerous aspect of the demonic is that many Christians who are ignorant of its hazards become involved. My experience has shown that ESP, astrology, mind dynamic or yoga meditation groups are Satan's main tools for deceiving the Christian. The devil is no respecter of persons. (*A Manual of Demonology and the Occult*, pg. *139 & 140*)

The dangerous trance-like altered state of mind creates an atmosphere conducive for the union of a demonic deity(ies) and a person:

> The altered state of mind is strangely similar to the trances and/or hypnotic states that spiritualist mediums, or other occultists experience when they are involved in occult activities... It has been a rather common experience in recent years to find middle class people becoming demon-

possessed through such seemingly harmless practices as yoga meditation for weight-reducing and mind-relaxing, mind growth or awareness exercises, tapping into "alpha wave levels," and mental exercises aimed at achieving positive or creative thinking. (pg. 43, 44)

However, without understanding the possibility of demonization, our courts are including yoga as a viable treatment for anger management. A startling newspaper headline dated January 23, 2004 reports, "Houston: Judge orders man to take yoga classes." The Judge Larry Standley issued the punishment of one year of probation to a man convicted of slapping his wife. Judge Standley also stated that he thought yoga would help with anger management (Temple Daily Telegram).

Since the fall of mankind, Satan has offered us a cheap imitation of God's perfect health and fitness plan. Indeed, throughout history, we have seen pagans practice the blasphemy of systematic, ritualistic dances performed to edify false gods for the purpose of achieving prosperity and good health. However, the practice is no longer limited to pagans.

Our western world has become infiltrated with eastern religion, integrated with mythical pagan gods. We are now witnessing ancient religious methods that have been repackaged to entice western, post-modern generations into accepting them as the latest and greatest way to health and prosperity.

Yoga is practiced in most every city throughout the land. No longer marginalized within Oriental provinces, it is now wildly popular and mainstreamed into our western culture at large. The dark secrets of ancient mysticism have found the light of day in the post-modern suburbs of America's small towns and towering cities, including the unguarded Christian churches.

One leader in the Catholic Church, Rev. Thomas Ryan, priest and author of *Prayer of Heart and Body Meditation, Yoga as a Christian Spiritual Practice,* has led many toward yoga. He personally led yoga retreats at the Kripalu Yoga Center in western Massachusetts. According to an article in "The Dallas Morning News" August 9, 2003, Ryan spoke highly of yoga as a connection to Christianity:

> There is a sense among some that this comes from Hinduism, but when one looks at yoga, it really belongs to world spirituality. [According to Ryan,] with an estimated 15 million practitioners in the United States.... [A]t least half of these people are coming to yoga from a Christian background.... There are an enormous number of people engaging in Eastern practices like yoga and meditation who need assistance making the points of connection with their Christian faith. (pg. 3G)

Neither the court's attempts to solve crime or the clergy's desire to assist in connecting with the Christian faith through yoga will improve either institution. In fact, yoga is proven to produce just the opposite effect.

Christian yoga is an oxymoron!

In the same article previously noted, a 22-year veteran of yoga exercises from Tulsa, Oklahoma, Laurette Willis, states that the feeling of euphoria she got from yoga left her vulnerable to psychic influences she believed to be demonic:

> "Yoga led me down a false rosy path... It opened the door to 20 years of involvement in the New Age movement." ...Willis says many yoga postures are based on ancient Hindu worship of the sun and moon as deities, and rejects the notion that they can be redeemed by putting a Christian spin on them. "Christian yoga is an oxymoron," she said. "It's like the fellow who says, 'I'm a Christian Buddhist.'" (The Dallas Morning News, Aug. 9, 2003 pg. 3G)

Yet, an article in the Fort Worth Star Telegram, May 5, 2007, claims that yoga and Christianity are compatible:

> Former 'Northern Exposure' star, [Janine Turner], joins with a Tarrant [County] fitness instructor to make 'Christoga,' a DVD that merges yoga with Bible verses.... "One day, it occurred to Cunningham – a [professing] Christian who teaches traditional yoga at a Southlake [Tx.] fitness center – that incorporating Bible verses into the meditation segment might help other Christians tone up spiritually as well as physically." [T]he women demonstrate yoga against a backdrop of crosses and candles. (pg. 8B)

The occult practice of clearing the mind

Why do so many professing Christians not understand that yoga is one way that demons are trafficking with humans? It's because the demonic interaction is done on a subconscious level within the trance state atmosphere. During the ritual of yoga, both voluntary and involuntary demon possession occurs within the practitioner.

According to demonology expert, Kent Philpott, in his book, A *Manual of Demonology and the Occult,* there are two kinds of demonization:

> Voluntary possession refers to a willingness on the part of a person to have demons or spirits enter him. A mediumistic trance is characteristic of a voluntary possession.... Possession of a person does not mean that a demon completely controls him all the time; it seems that a demon may reside passively in a person and manifest itself at different times. Involuntary demonization refers to some kind of influence of a person by a demon, perhaps resulting in an obsession.... Demons cannot indwell a person against his will. So involuntary demonization refers to a person being influenced by the demonic without any conscious or willing yielding to the demonic on his part. Demonization, particularly the indwelling by a demon, can occur only as a person yields to evil spirits or sin. (pg. 116& 117)

Raphael Gasson, a former spiritualist medium says, "Possession can occur during trances, meditation, hypnosis, séances, and involvement in various occult practices. Demons want a passive mind, a blank mind in a person, so that they may make an entrance. Passivity and a blanking out of mental thoughts and images are very characteristic of many occult practices" (pg. 117).

It is sin that opens the door to demonic influence. Voluntary exposure to the occult is sin. Involuntary exposure to the occult is sin. The results are the same. "It is clear that possession occurs to people who willingly yield themselves as slaves to demons, either through exposure to the occult, demonic doctrine, or actual Satan worship" (pg. 117).

The Bible teaches that demons do possess people (Acts 16:16-18, 19:11-16). Furthermore, Jesus taught that a person delivered from demon possession can even be repossessed (Matt. 12:43-45). The demon was cast out, but found no rest. It returned to find the person spiritually empty and thereby re-entered the soul of the man. Thanks to Jesus' work on the cross, as Christians we have the authority to cast out demons (Matt. 10:1).

Those of you who are now taking yoga classes, unaware of the danger, may testify of its amazing influence. You may be convinced of the emotional, spiritual, and physical benefits. You may feel stronger, more in control of your life and even more spiritually attuned. You have not realized how, in a relatively short time, the powerful threads of the ancient incantations, along with the postures and the challenging enigmas of the *mantras*, are working their magic into the very fabric of your being.

These mysterious words (*mantras*) and puzzles (*sutras*) are euphemisms for an occult language and twisted logic that defines yoga. If we are mystified and confused by the esoteric meanings of terms embedded in this practice, then we should expect that the confusing language of the New Age movement would have the same effect. The confusion is purposeful. ✝

Yoga's New Age vocabulary confuses and ensnares many unsuspecting Christians in its terminology. New Age believers know that their ideas are more agreeable when language is manipulated to conform to the mindset of the target audience. Altering meaning by using familiar diction and syntax is a common rhetorical method of persuasion.

The name of God is the most widely misunderstood term. All religions outside of Judeo-Christianity interpret God to be an "energy source" or a "universal consciousness." But in truth, God is a personal being. His name is Yahweh, LORD, the God of Abraham, Isaac and Jacob. He exists in three persons: the Father, Son, and Holy Spirit.

Let's take a look at the meanings of false religious terms and language. These should be taken as a warning to the unsuspecting.

The New Age/Eastern mystic vocabulary and definitions:

God – An impersonal energy force, called Brahman, "universal consciousness," or "higher self," a state of enlightenment or one's personal understanding. To the eastern mystical religions, "God" can be male/female/mother/father/god or goddess.

The Hindus serve a pantheon of 330 million gods. Chief among the Hindu gods are <u>Brahma</u>, "...*Shiva* [Siva], a fierce figure representing both the creative and destructive sides of divinity as well as the ideal of yogic meditation, and *Vishnu*, who incarnates himself many times through history in order to bring the message of salvation to man."

Many animals are worshiped as gods. The elements are also worshiped including mother earth, called Gia, the sun, the moon and the stars – in fact all of nature is worshiped as "God" (*Comparing Christianity with World Religions*).

<u>Christ</u> – An incarnation or avatar, a messiah, or a messenger. According to *Comparing Christianity with the Cults*, eastern mystics believe that Christ is among a long line of "Masters" who evolved himself into divinity in the same way as Buddha or Shankacharya, or Yogananda, or other recognized divine leaders.

However, the New Age Movement is looking for one greater than these to come to earth and usher in the New World Order which will include the One World Religious system. This greater man, the yoga gurus' claim, will solve the world's economic, political, and religious problems.

This man for whom the New Agers are waiting is the Antichrist, described in II Thessalonians 2:3&4. Those within the Unity Religion believe that Krishna of the Hindus is the same as and equal to the Christos of the Greeks and the Messiah of the Hebrews. "This Christ or perfect man idea existing eternally in divine mind is the true spiritual higher-self of every individual" (*Comparing Christianity with the Cults*).

<u>Holy Spirit</u> – "All-pervading power of Divine love" ... "an all-pervading energy"... "Kundalini is the spiritual mother of every individual".... "When this Kundalini rises it connects you to the all-pervading power"... "which is an ocean of knowledge as well as an ocean of bliss".... "So whatever mistakes you have committed in the past are forgiven and instead you get your self-realization as a blessing" (www. sahajayoga.org pg.4).

<u>Angels</u> – Referred to as masters, gods, spirit guides, one's higher-self, the self, walk-ins, inner-guides, or muses. The Bible, God's Holy Word, exposes these entities as demons, evil spirits, devils, and "angels of light" disobedient to God. The Bible warns us of these deceiving spirits (Deut. 8:10-12) and the LORD tells us never to bow down in worship to these renegade angels. Nor are we ever to bow to God's own angels (Rev. 19:10). Unfortunately, the yoga practitioner does indeed bow down to angels. Worshipping through occult body language brings demonic angels into relationship with mankind.

<u>Born again</u> – eastern mysticism and New Age religion calls this rebirth, and it occurs through the lie of reincarnation. We receive instantaneous "enlightenment" or understanding that we are all one with the all-pervading soul. We learn that we are God. The New Age movement describes being born again as "The clear vision of what we are, 'the divine or inner light, and the god within.' We need not go elsewhere. All may say, at the moment of the awakening, 'I am the way'." (*Comparing Christianity with the Cults*).

This awakening is often described as Kundalini, a Hindu term meaning "serpent power." It occurs in a moment when the yoga recipient is transformed by the serpent's hot breath and light and begins receiving a greater spiritual awareness of occult knowledge.

Enlightenment: Wisdom that is obtained by becoming "one" with the "Universal World Soul." The word yoga is defined in English as "yoked or union" and means that the yogi is yoked to the divine "World Soul" that imparts knowledge and "enlightenment." According to eastern religious practice, occult knowledge is transferred to the yoga practitioner by the serpent Kundalini.

Heaven – The ultimate utopia. Achieved through works of perpetual deaths and rebirths, considered to be attained only after one has obtained perfect wisdom. Heaven is the reward of ultimate achievement of self-perfected man, the evolutionary god. New Age believers claim that we can reach God by our own works and methods; therefore, we become our own salvation. "It is the gradual movement from Matter to Mind, and then to Super Mind. Once we reach the Super Mind, we reach the union with the divine" (Comparing Christianity with the Cults).

Hell – The New Age denies its existence. In fact, many false religions of the world deny hell exists. According to, Comparing Christianity with the Cults the doctrine of Spiritualism claims "Hell does not exist and never will. All spirit people of wisdom, knowledge, and love know there is no hell and no devil. No resurrection-no judgment." Christian Science teaches, "Hell is mortal belief, error, lust, remorse, hatred, revenge, sin, sickness, death . . . that which worketh abomination or make it a lie. No final judgment awaits mortals."

The *Bhagavad-Gita As It Is* claims misery and martyrdom is the only life that is to be experienced on earth. To enjoy this life too much will cause you to go to Hell.

> ...perplexed by various anxieties and bound by a network of illusions, one becomes too strongly attached to sense enjoyment and falls down into hell. (pg. 239)

Conversely, Jesus declares, "I have come that they may have life, and that they may have it more abundantly" (John 10:10). Eastern mysticism doctrine declares that karma, the 'law of the deed,' of sowing and reaping, is allied with transmigration (reincarnation). Karma defines the afterlife as the result of sins and rewards for good behavior.

Comparing Christianity with the World Religions reveals that the end of life for the Buddhist is Nirvana, which literally means 'blowing out,' a state of transcendent permanence. For the Hindu, the end is the 'unimaginable abyss of Brahman.'

Reality - Yoga mystics create their own reality, whereby the light (truth) is found in the ancient Hindu holy scriptures of the *Bhagavad-Gita*, which includes the Vedas. According to the Vedas, no one can enter the heavenly planets without believing in their philosophies. A demon is one who does not believe in the "created reality" of the Vedas and doesn't believe all his wealth comes only from his past lives, good deeds, and that his present life is preparation for the next reincarnated life.

The Jews and Christians are thereby defined as demons. Demonizing others is reality to eastern mystics. Reincarnation along with "self" mastery techniques and illusionary <u>reality</u> sum up the occult world religions.

Hindu holy writings teach that by using yoga meditation, one can break the ties to this earth and the illusions of this world and be enlightened to Krishna. Krishna is the earthly avatar or god of the Vedas. Krishna is <u>reality</u> and is said to be merciful, according to the Vedas, because all demons (Jews and Christians) killed by the supreme lord Krishna will be liberated!

> Sometimes the asuras [demons] are killed by the supreme lord. This killing is also good for them, for in Vedic literature we find that anyone killed by the supreme lord is liberated. (*Bhagavad-Gita As It Is*, pg. 242)

The Bible is the inerrant Word of God. Hell is real. Jesus Christ Himself holds the keys to the bottomless pit (Rev. 20:1). It is reserved for Satan and his followers. All who refuse God's Truth and salvation through the blood of Jesus Christ are destined for Hell. We have been given the power to choose life and death, blessing and cursing (Deut. 30:19). God does not send mankind to hell. However, those who reject God's provision of Jesus Christ freely choose eternal separation from God (Heb. 9:15).

The major deception is the blurring between the Truth of Jesus Christ and the lie of Satan. The demonic spirits are working overtime to bring forth chaos and confusion on several levels.

New Age lie exalts self-will

The "serpent power" spirit inherent in all false religions, including Hinduism and Buddhism, is the spirit of antichrist. We know that Satan is more cunning than any of God's creatures (Gen.3:1). He will adapt and change his form, moving wherever he can to seduce us into accepting his lies. His New Age lie is that we should exalt self-will over God's will. Those who believe the lie commit the sin of rebellion.

Today, a middle-aged generation is sharing their occult yoga wisdom with new generations to keep the spirit of yoga alive and exponentially increasing. The danger, again, is that so many within these generations are unaware of yoga's profound influence. They idealistically expect to preserve their own personal disciplines and religion and make no connection between a yoga class and the worship of its gods.

This deceived generation simply focuses on the physical benefits of yoga, which they see as a kind of magic salvation from obesity, lethargy, stress and disease. They are taught that anyone can share in this works-oriented salvation with its marvelous stretching exercises. Without thinking of the implications, these generations turn a deaf ear and a blind eye to the obvious religious rituals of the popularized yoga class.

When Christians can become so thoroughly deceived, tricked into compromising the Word of God, and question the sovereignty of Jesus Christ, Satan has succeeded in seducing them into walking down the "broad path." We must beware of this way of walking. Matthew's Gospel gives us clear warning:

"Enter by the narrow gate; for wide is the gate
and broad is the way that leads to destruction,
and there are many who go in by it. Because
narrow is the gate, and difficult is the way which
leads to life, there are few who find it." (Matt.
7:13-14, NKJ)

If we enter the wide gate into yoga's deceptive religious
rituals, we will walk down a broad incremental path of
destruction. At the end of the path, we will find that we
have been serving a new master: self, not God. God's Word
teaches just the opposite: "Trust in the LORD with all thine
heart, and lean not unto thine own understanding" (Prov.
3:5, KJV).

As Christians, we must pray for discernment. We must
be able to separate the counterfeit from the real. How can
we spot the counterfeit? When the experts compare money
(bills) to identify the counterfeit, they don't first examine
the counterfeit. Instead, they examine the real thing. After
spending much time looking at the real thing, the experts can
easily spot the counterfeit.

In the same way that the experts focus on real money,
we need to spend time focusing on Jesus Christ face to face,
enjoying His presence, reading His Word, and following Him.
Then we will easily discern the counterfeit gods of Buddhism,
Hinduism, Islam, and other New Age religions.

The Bible calls for us to seek God's face in prayer and
to repent of our sins, so we can receive the blessing:

> If My people, who are called by My name, shall
> humble themselves, and pray, and seek My face,
> and turn from their wicked ways; then will I hear
> from heaven, and will forgive their sin, and will
> heal their land. (II Chronicles 7:14, NKJ)

God says that He would not have us remain ignorant (1 Thessalonians 4:13), but shows us all mysteries:

> And He said to them, "To you it has been given
> to know the mystery of the kingdom of God..."
> (Mark 4:11a, NKJ)

The Apostle Paul teaches in Colossians that we are to be encouraged and knit together in love, to have the full assurance of understanding, and to know the mystery of God, both of the Father and of Christ, in whom are hidden all the treasures of wisdom and knowledge (Colossians 2:2b-3, NKJ).

You are God's chosen child. You are called by His name. Do not allow yourself to be yoked with the counterfeit religions of yoga. Yoke yourself with Jesus Christ, for He will give you His wisdom. You are not Satan's pawn. Do not live as though you are posturing yourself upon the chessboard of compromise.

Chapter 3

Exposing the Heart of Lucifer

How you are fallen from heaven, O Lucifer, son of the morning! How you are cut down to the ground, you who weakened the nations! For you have said in your heart: 'I will ascend into heaven; I will exalt my throne above the stars of God; I will also sit on the mount of the congregation on the farthest sides of the north; I will ascend above the heights of the clouds, I will be like the Most High' (Isaiah 14:12-14, NKJ).

> And war broke out in heaven: Michael and his angels fought with the dragon; [Satan] and the dragon and his angels fought, but they did not prevail, nor was a place found for them in heaven any longer. So the great dragon was cast out, that serpent of old, called the Devil and Satan, who deceives the whole world; he was cast to the earth, and his angels were cast out with him.... "Therefore rejoice, O heavens, and you who dwell in them! Woe to the inhabitants of the earth and the sea! For the devil has come down to you, having great wrath, because he knows that he has a short time." (Rev. 12:7, 9 & 12, NKJ)

In his book, *One World*, author Tal Brooke states how utterly spectacular Lucifer's transformation from the most beautiful and anointed of God's created angels, to Satan, the Great Dragon must have been:

When "Lucifer fell and became Satan, the Father
of Lies"... Satan became the spiritual equivalent
of a black hole. His evil became all consuming
and his hostility to God, after he transformed,
became total.

His footprints, however, can be seen across time,
across human history, as the great adversary of
God who is the architect of the Great Lie, and
the secret mystery religion upon which it rides.
(pg. 216)

What is the Great Lie? The great lie is that mankind
can master itself. Lucifer, the father of lies, is the author of
self-mastery. When Lucifer turned from God's supremacy,
he initiated the sin of rebellion by acting under his own
authority. Lucifer made his choice to depend solely on his
own reprobate mind for guidance. Therefore, Lucifer and all
those he influences are "... always learning, and never able
to come to the knowledge of the truth" (II Tim. 3:7).

Thinking himself wise, Lucifer actually became a fool
because he chose to rebel against God. For his deadly and
foolish action, he was punished, cast out from God's presence
and separated from his Creator. Now he lives apart from the
TRUTH. He is full of pride and there is no TRUTH in him
(John 8:44).

Lucifer wasn't cast out of heaven alone. He took one-
third of the angelic hosts with him. "His tail drew a third of
the stars of heaven and threw them to the earth" (Rev. 12:4).
Stars are a metaphor for angels in Revelation 1:20.

The angels did not keep their proper domain but left their own abode (Jude vs. 6)..."wandering stars of whom is reserved the blackness of darkness forever" (vs. 13). Satan and his angels, full of pride, are upon the face of the earth serving themselves rather than God.

The idea of *self-mastery* is spawned from unadulterated pride, the first of the seven deadly sins followed by gluttony, sloth, greed, envy, wrath, and lust. *Pride* is not to be understood as the expression of gratitude for honor and achievement, but rather as presumptuous ambition, haughty egotism, and self-serving rebellion.

How ironic that the message of eastern mystic religion is clothed in claims of passivity and humility. The followers of Hinduism and Buddhism declare that their roots are deeply embedded in humility. But don't be deceived. Their roots are deeply embedded in pride. Pride is the seed, root, and fruit of all counterfeit religions.

Lucifer's declarations

The Old Testament prophet, Isaiah, reveals the heart of Lucifer, who seeks to glorify himself. Listen to Lucifer's five declarations of self-serving pride. They are sometimes referred to as his five "I wills."

> For you [Lucifer] said in your heart:
> 'I will ascend into heaven.
> I will exalt my throne above the stars of God;
> I will also sit on the mount of the congregation
> on the farthest side of the north;

I will ascend above the heights of the clouds,
I will be like the Most High.' (Isaiah 14:13-14)

Lucifer [Satan] manages to effect a so-called triumph in his effort to be like the Most High. Jesus calls him the "ruler of this world" (John 12:31). As ruler, he makes decisions that are motivated by self-serving pride and are in direct opposition to God's commandments, thereby demonstrating self-mastery.

From the beginning Lucifer [Satan] has served as his own god. He glorifies himself and has his way in the world of darkness. The heart of Lucifer burns with unbridled ambition to fulfill the five "I wills." His greatest passion is to be worshiped as God. Lucifer is the imitator of God. He has orchestrated deceptive religious movements to fulfill his evil desire to be worshiped.

Lucifer, the father of *self-will*, is the power behind the forces of yoga and all the movements that spring from eastern mysticism. You must be asking, "How can we claim that Lucifer's act of rebellion is the origin of occult religions?"

We rely on the words of the Holy Bible. There are clear connections between the teachings of eastern mysticism and the Bible's description of Lucifer's motives and his activity in the world. Thousands of years ago, Isaiah warned of eastern mystical idol worship.

> Surely [LORD] You have rejected and forsaken your people, the house of Jacob, because they are filled [with customs] from the east and with soothsayers [who foretell] like the Philistines; also they strike hands and make pledges and

agreements with the children of aliens.... Their land also is full of idols... (Isaiah 2:6 & 2:8a, Amplified)

The "house of Jacob" means Israel (Gen. 32:28). Isaiah is confessing to God that the Israelites have acted like pagans. Today, pagan philosophies are still considered alien to the Word of God, and they include the teachings of Muslims, Buddhists, and Hindus. Isaiah's words are prophetic and profound, and they apply today in the same way as when he spoke them for the first time to the disobedient children of God centuries ago.

Most of us observe God's warnings when He tells us not to practice divination by seeking wisdom from fortune telling, psychic readings, horoscopes, and speaking to the dead, but do we know not to join the yoga class at the local community center? There are many who would never call the psychic hot line, yet they would haphazardly practice yoga, thus unknowingly practicing the same abominations of other nations (Deut. 18:10). The Bible clearly forbids mystical eastern practices such as divination.

"Divination" means to explore the unknown by occult means. Yoga clearly engages in these practices. Yoga is the act of exploring mysteries of the unknown of the so-called *divine self* through the practice of *union with occult enlightenment.*

Yoga adepts explore the unknown mysteries of self, seeking wisdom within. The Word of God, however, gives us the only authentic Wisdom.

For the LORD gives Wisdom; from His mouth come knowledge and understanding... (Proverbs 2:6, NKJ)

...I [Jesus] will give you a mouth and wisdom which all your adversaries will not be able to contradict or resist. (Luke 21:15, NKJ)

There are many references to wisdom in the Word of God, but nowhere does God say we possess wisdom outside of Him. Nowhere does He say we can look within ourselves, void of His Word, and find true wisdom. Yet the yoga masters make prideful claims in possessing such wisdom.

The yoga master's goal, like Lucifer's goal, is to serve *self*. Lucifer's egocentric logic feeds the desires of the fleshly self. The flesh, full of itself, overpowers the spirit, and true worship of God ends and communion with Lucifer begins. Jesus warns us to stay alert. There is a battle between the flesh and the spirit. "Watch and pray, lest you enter into temptation. The spirit indeed is willing, but the flesh is weak" (Matt. 26:41).

Yoga – the forbidden fruit

Adam and Eve thought the forbidden fruit looked good, but they were gravely mistaken. In spite of God's instruction not to eat from the tree of the knowledge of good and evil (Gen.2:17), they exalted their own will. They trusted in their own eyes to guide them and were deceived. They did not stay alert, they believed Lucifer's great lie which led them to question God's Word. Lucifer [as the serpent] asks, "Has God indeed said?" (Gen. 3:1).

Lucifer's mantra continues to be chanted throughout our world. Its echo is carried in the air. Satan, after all, is called "The prince of the power of the air, the spirit who now works in the sons of disobedience..." (Eph. 2:2). His lies are as deadly as the anthrax virus. Even more so today Satan is transmitting his lies through the airwaves.

During yoga performance, the airwaves explode with a body language of worship to the gods that carry the deadly virus of lies into the atmosphere. Yoga worshipers are exposed to and ingest the deadly spores as subliminal messages, and their souls assimilate the disease. Subconsciously, their minds are infected with the lies and ultimately the disease manifests in varying degrees of biblical compromise leading practitioners to ask their "divine" selves, "Has God indeed said?" (Gen. 3:1)

By the inspiration of the Holy Spirit, Paul warns Colossians of the deadly lies:

> Now this I say lest anyone should deceive you...
> As you therefore have received Christ Jesus the
> LORD, so walk in Him, rooted and built up in
> Him and established in the faith, as you have
> been taught, abounding in it with thanksgiving.
> Beware lest anyone cheat you through philosophy
> and empty deceit, according to the tradition of
> men, according to the basic principles of the
> world, and not according to Christ. (Colossians
> 2:4a, 6-8, NKJ)

Unfortunately through yoga practices, antichrist spirits are summoned into the practitioner's presence where demons consume the sacrifices of their worship. Within the spirit realm these demons are the audience of the yoga practitioners who are deceived by the seemingly innocent yoga stretches and poses.

Sacrifices made to demons, not to God!

In the book of Corinthians, Paul explains that behind acts of idol worship lurks a receptive demon:

> What am I trying to say? Am I saying that the idols to whom the pagans bring sacrifices are real gods and that these sacrifices are of some value? No, not at all. What I am saying is that these sacrifices are offered to demons, not to God. And I don't want any of you to be partners with demons. (I Corinthians 10:19-20, New Living Bible)

Paul is explaining that when Christians practice ancient postures that are rooted in pagan religious rituals, they open the door to demons that are lurking in and behind these ceremonies. Demons who are receiving the practitioner's sacrifice of worship are consuming these sacrifices for their own egocentric appetites. They accept the offering of worship as if the purpose is to honor them through yoga. Therefore, the yoga practitioner has become a living sacrifice, offered to demons rather than to God.

Once Satan's demons are evoked through yoga's ancient sacrificial rituals, the door is opened to the union of man with demons or so-called gods. Remember that the word *yoga* means *union* or *yoking*, the act of becoming "one."

As Christians, despite our hearts' and minds' desires to worship only God through Jesus Christ, we are in danger of committing spiritual adultery by evoking the union (yoga) of "oneness" with other gods and by offering a sacrifice of worship to them. The heart of Lucifer is gratified by spiritual adultery, but Lucifer is certainly not the one to gratify. He is not our Master. We cannot serve two masters. ✶✶✶

✶ We **cannot** sacrifice ourselves to idols with our body language speaking out the ancient Hindu and Buddhist religious rituals at the same time that we offer ourselves to God as a holy, set a part, and dedicated sacrifice to Him. Paul confirms the impossibility of maneuvering between these two extremes:

> ✶ You cannot drink the cup of the LORD and the cup of demons; you cannot partake of the LORD's table and of the table of demons. (I Cor. 10:21, NKJ)

The New Age, on the other hand, proclaims that all religions and sacrifices are acceptable. Leading the New Age, heralded by millions, Satan seduces his followers to reject the truth of the cross. In his book, *Dark Secrets of the New Age*, Texe Marrs explains the core of New Age belief:

> The essence of the New Age religious doctrine is that man is neither sinful nor evil, and that Jesus' sacrifice on the cross was meaningless and futile. Man did not need a Savior to atone for sin, says the New Age, because man has for millennia been inevitably evolving toward perfection and godhood. (pg. 13)

Throughout the ages, Satan's schemes have spread through occult practices which have coalesced today into the New Age religion. Proponents of New Age beliefs capitalize upon the great lie by systematically teaching that all individuals can "evolve" or "actualize" into becoming God's equal. Becoming God's equal is Lucifer's heart.

Yoga declares – "I AM"

Through yoga postures, New Age believers say to themselves and to anyone who will listen, "I am God." Their misguided revelation comes through believing the lie of the serpent and by "awakening" a memory of personal godhood that has supposedly been lost.

Throughout their enlightenment process, yogi gurus chant the words, "Om" or "Aum" which is interpreted in English as "I AM" (Marrs, pg. 114). With each utterance these yogis mock the LORD God. Yogi gurus say, "It is possible to enter into relationship with Isvara (Universal World Soul), to contact him, by reciting the sound Om" (*The Heart of Yoga*, pg.129).

Almighty God is the only *One* with authority to identify Himself as "I AM."

> And God said to Moses, "I AM WHO I AM." And He said, "Thus you shall say to the children of Israel, I Am has sent me to you.... This is My name forever, and this is My memorial to all generations." (Exodus 3:14&15, NKJ)

History is full of examples of those who declare, either openly or in veiled phrases, that they are God. Rene Descartes (1596-1650), French philosopher and mathematician said "I think, therefore, I am." Also, Shirley MacLaine, from her New Age mindset, asserts "I am God."

Millions of yoga practitioners chant, "I Am." The Word of God prophesied that this Antichrist spirit would arise. Jesus tells us that there will be many antichrists who will proclaim, "I Am and there is none before me." These people are false christs:

> "For false christs and false prophets will rise
> and show great signs and wonders to deceive,
> if possible, even the elect." (Matt. 24:24, NKJ)

Like Lucifer, the yoga practitioners are saying, "I will be as God!" The New Testament proclaims the heresy of Antichrist who masquerades as God. Apostle Paul prophetically announces the man of sin's appearance on earth:

> Let no one deceive you by any means; for that day [the coming of the LORD Jesus Christ and the gathering together with Him, II Thess. 2:1] will not come unless the falling away comes first, and the man of sin is revealed, the son of perdition, who opposes and exalts himself above all that is called God or that is worshipped, so that he sits as God in the temple of God, showing himself that he is God. (II Thess. 2:3&4, NKJ)

Lucifer is Satan, the shining one, the angel of light, the Devil, the Antichrist spirit. He is exposed in the heart of yoga.

Chapter 4

Yoga – A Sign Language to the gods

Yoga is disguised as merely a physical exercise, but it includes sign language rituals that involve the whole body, the hands, arms, feet, legs, head, neck, back and torso. Hand sign languages are called *mudras*.

According to yoga theory, your hand gestures can bring forth occult power from within yourself through mystic positions. The book, *Mudras: Yoga in Your Hands*, by Gertrud Hirschi, describes the ancient prayer language of yoga and admits that mudras carry with them mystic powers using seals and symbols:

> Mudra is a term with many meanings. It is used to signify a gesture, a mystic position of the hands, a seal, or even a symbol. However, there are eye positions, body postures, and breathing techniques that are called mudras. (Hirschi pg.2)

The mudras speak into the mystical spiritual realm. The ancient yogi masters intended the sign language to be a way of entry for gods in the spiritual realm to come into their flesh. According to *Living Yoga*, the yoga mat becomes an altar cloth upon which the yogis practice their rituals to obtain knowledge:

Ritual, the use of symbols and meaningful actions
fired by intention toward a specific purpose, can
afford a means of entry into sacred time and
space, an access to meaning in life and the tattoo
of daily routine. (pg. 245)

Knowledge and power can be accessed by the
intentional use of such symbols. "Symbols are the language
of the unconscious, just as words are the language of the
conscious mind" (pg. 245). According to yoga advocates, the
choreographed body languages, symbols, and gestures of the
hands are believed to move the practitioner into another time
and space that affords a means of entry into the spirit realm.
Once inside this "sacred" spirit realm, the practitioner can
commune with and access the occult knowledge and power
of the ancient gods.

Specific yoga sign languages are part of a dance ritual.
The collective choreographed yoga dance is called "Bharat
Natyum," and is solely intended to bring man into the
manifested presence of the gods. "The different hand gestures
or mudras, are used to tell the many different tales that are
associated with each of the gods" (www.courses.rochester.
edu/muller-ortega).

The worship and communion with the gods is depicted
in the Hindu Temple dances. Indian classical dances to the
gods have been performed for thousands of years as the art
of temple worship. Within yoga there are many different
choreographed dance postures all of which pay homage to
the Hindu gods:

The dancer who dissolves her identity in the
rhythm and music makes her body the medium
for the experience and expression of the spirit.
(www.trivenidance.org/dance.html)

These ancient yoga (union) dances performed on a yoga
mat contain the same choreographed body language of the
current day yoga rituals. With each posture, mudra, and
mantra, the designated gods or goddesses are receiving the
disciplined practitioner as holy and consecrated unto them.

We are the temple of the Holy Spirit!

✳ Many unsuspecting people, while professing to be
Christians and claiming to worship the One True Living God,
are actually stretching out their bodies in a sign language of
worship to other gods. Our bodies are not our own, and we
must not be led into spiritual apathy or into the greater danger
of spiritual adultery. We are to glorify God in our bodies, not
defile our bodies by yoking ourselves with other gods:

> Or do you not know that your body is the temple
> of the Holy Spirit who is in you, whom you have
> from God, and you are not your own? For you
> were bought at a price; therefore glorify God in
> your body and in your spirit, which are God's.
> (I Cor.6:19 & 20, NKJ)

Clearly the yoga dancer welcomes voluntary demonization.
Even the yoga masters confess that the postures of the dance
will open the physical body to channel the spirits. As God's
children, we are forbidden to use the temple of the Holy Spirit
as a playground for demonic activities:

"There shall not be found among you anyone who makes his son or his daughter pass through the fire [made a sacrifice], or one who practices witchcraft, or a soothsayer, or one who interprets omens, or a sorcerer, or one who conjures spells, or a medium, or a spiritist, or one who calls up the dead." (Deut.18:10-11, NKJ)

To become a **medium** for the Hindu "divine" spirits is an abomination to God Almighty. As the yoga dancer achieves union with the gods, the abomination is complete. Yoga cannot possibly serve God. The yoga dance Kuchipudi, serves a counterfeit Christ, Krishna.

> The dance focuses on the worship of Krishna. Kuchipudi is a dramatization of the story of one of the Lord Krishna's wives. (www.trivenidance. org/dance.html)

Krishna or any so-called god is mankind's adversary. In fact, they are demonic beings. When the yoga dancers offer themselves as a living sacrifice, bowing and giving worship to these gods, this abomination angers the LORD.

> "They provoked Him to jealousy with foreign gods; with abominations they provoked Him to anger." (Deuteronomy 32:16, NKJ)

God is jealous over His covenant children and their well being (Gen. 17). Regardless of the intentions of the yoga practitioner's heart, it is impossible to worship the One True God through this pagan ritual.

Yoga is Hinduism

✗ Many gurus state emphatically that **there is no Hinduism without yoga and no yoga without Hinduism.** These kinds of statements coming from the experienced yogi teachers should prove that practicing yoga is indeed bowing to foreign gods. No one is saying it louder or more clearly than the yogi masters themselves.

Yoga does not glorify the God of the Bible, but instead, gives glory to other gods including the Hindu god, Siva:

> We perform japa, meditation and yoga each day... It is the mystical mental, physical and devotional exercise that enables us to dance with Siva... Once we begin to move with the sacred flow that surrounds us... We are then gracefully, in unrestrained surrender, dancing with Siva. (www.adishaki.org/miscellaneous/ battle_of_armageddon.htm, pg. 11 of 41)

Still some persist in arguing: How can it possibly be wrong to do yoga exercise to strengthen and tone and beautify our bodies? Being strong and slender and healthy is a good thing, isn't it? Of course the answer is yes, but the answer to yoga is No! Yoga is not about getting physically fit.

It was designed to seduce us into becoming a living sacrifice to demons, serving the false gods of this world, consecrating ourselves to Satan rather than God. The word "consecrate" means "set apart as holy; make or declare sacred for religious use" (*Webster's New World Dictionary, Third College Edition*). So for yoga practitioners to perform the sacred dance means they are in fact making themselves a holy, dedicated sacrifice to demons.

Clearly, there is an awesome power contained in the dance, which was created to worship our God, otherwise Satan would not have hijacked the practice of worship to further his kingdom.

Dance for Joy!

Our Jewish ancestors understood the power of dance. According to the book *Dancing for Joy: A Biblical Approach to Praise and Worship*, by Murray Silberling, "Philosophically, the Jewish people have always connected sacred dance to their identity as God's chosen people" (pg.15).

The purpose of the Davidic dance is to worship Yahweh. The ancient choreographed movements *invoke* (to call upon God) God Almighty, the God of Abraham, Isaac, and Jacob.

The choreographed dance of our LORD God is declarative in nature. Through dancing in praise and worship, considerable spiritual warfare is accomplished. When we declare the true words of Scripture and celebrate our freedom in Jesus Christ, our enemies are scattered. The power of the Word of God is declared with each faith-filled step of our choreographed body language, and with each word the demons tremble:

> Even the demons believe – and tremble! (James 2:19b, NKJ)

Picture all the Israelites after their deliverance, vibrant and strong, singing and dancing on the shore of the Red Sea as they thanked God for their deliverance from their Egyptian slavery. God's will for us is that our bodies, as well as our souls, are healthy and prosperous.

Beloved, I pray that you may prosper in all things and be in health, just as your soul prospers. (3 John 2, NKJ)

Within the last few centuries there has been an increase of various sects of the Christian Church regaining their religious and cultural roots in Jewish worship. We have seen these churches demonstrate their appreciation of the brotherhood they share with the Jewish people and their nation. In his noted book, Silberling documents that these Christians understand that they are grafted into Israel by the blood of Christ, and they now regard with respect the relationship they have with the Orthodox and the Messianic Jew:

> It is not surprising that the greater the attachment of the Church to its Jewish roots, the richer its biblical faith. (*Dancing for Joy*, pg. 22)

Consider the Messianic Jewish movement to return to their cultural roots. In 1967, they were appropriately shocked into prioritizing their lives, putting God where He belongs, foremost in their hearts and minds.

In 1967, during the dramatic Six-Day War, Jerusalem became a Jewish city, the capital of the Jewish State. During the Yom Kippur War the new generation of Jewish believers, called Messianic Jews, were determined to get back to their roots and maintain their Jewish identity in worship. Their identity included claiming the prophetic biblical promises to Israel and incorporating the Davidic worship of dance (*Dancing for Joy*, pg.23).

There is a powerful release of the Spirit of God
when a community harmonizes together in praise
and worship... your congregation can experience
a fresh spiritual revival through dance. (*Dancing
for Joy*, pg. 25-26)

Jesus Christ Himself was Jewish and He is our life source
referred to in John 15:5. Christians should certainly become
partakers in the richness and fullness of Israel, God's first
fruits. Through the ritual of the Davidic dance that praises and
worships our God, we will find a glorious joy. Furthermore,
as we perform that dance of joy, we will demonstrate humility
and reverence for our awesome God.

The Lord calls His children to return to their roots. He
desires to reshape us into what He originally intended for us,
which is to *take off the old man and put on the new* (Col. 3:9-10).
He desires that we look like Him in our actions and that we are
like Him in our thoughts so that we can enjoy the abundant
life now. We are called to be the purified Bride waiting for
the Bridegroom. We are called to dance for joy and to become
strong in good health, both physically and spiritually:

"Then shall the virgin [the Bride] rejoice in the
dance." (Jeremiah 31:13, ref. 33:11, NKJ)

Biblical dance has been given to us as a way to worship
our God and at the same time bring good health and joy to
our spirits, souls, and bodies. Not only will we maintain
strong, supple bodies, but we will also express great joy and
health-giving laughter as we move in Christ into the Holy of
Holies, from praise to worship until we see His glory.

When we practice any form of worshipful rituals, whether
it be prayers, praise or dance, we enter beyond the veil of the

unseen spiritual realm or heavenly places. The greeter on the "other side" will either be the One True God, the Creator of the heavens and the earth, the LORD Jesus Christ, or Satan, the master of the kingdom of darkness.

The Hindus and the Buddhists use yoga's choreographed sign languages to enter beyond the veil to worship the false gods of this world:

> Expressional dance uses a complex and stylized system of gesture and facial expression to praise and tell the stories of the gods and goddesses in the Hindu pantheon. Dance is an art form that consecrates the body. (www.trivenidance.org/dance.html)

Because of the original sin of mankind, we are all born into the kingdom of darkness, where Satan is "the god of this world," and as unbelievers, we are blind to the truth:

> Satan, who is the god of this world, has blinded the minds of those who don't believe. They are unable to see the glorious light of the Good News. They don't understand this message about the glory of Christ, who is the exact likeness of God. (II Cor. 4:4, NLT)

If we are born again in the spirit through the blood of Jesus Christ, then and only then are we transported (conveyed) from Satan's kingdom of darkness into God's Kingdom of Light:

> [We are]...giving thanks to the Father who has qualified us to be partakers of the inheritance

of the saints in the light. He has delivered us from the power of darkness and conveyed us into the Kingdom of the Son of His love, in whom we have redemption through His blood, the forgiveness of sins. (Col. 1:12-14, NKJ)

Therefore, when we bow, pray, praise, and worship, in accordance with God's Word, we can be assured that we have come boldly into the "throne of grace" and have been received by the Holy Spirit into the very presence of God (Hebrews 4:16).

Danger abounds when "born again" Christians practice yoga whether through their own defiance or out of sheer ignorance. Yoga literally works as a key to open the door to the spiritual realm of the kingdom of darkness. The yoga practitioner is consecrated within the posturing that bows to and worships specific deities.

Now the battle ensues. Yoga dancing Christians, whose spirits are cleansed by the blood of Jesus and spiritually dwell in the Kingdom of God, open the door to the kingdom of darkness and give place to the devil. Through idol worship they evoke a union with the gods of this world.

Consequences seen and unseen bombard the spirit, mind, and body of the yoga dancer and occur not only in the physical realm but in the spiritual realm as well. Sign languages to the gods will bring adverse consequences of destruction. Therefore, turn away from yoga, a sign language to the gods.

you can skip to Ch 10 as I dont imagine you do these next things!

Chapter 5

The Satanic Mechanics of Yoga

The mechanics of both <u>mystical and physical yoga will open the door</u> to occult powers. According to yoga advocate and author, Gertrud Hirschi, in her book, *Mudras: Yoga in Your Hands*, like a **medium** or **channeler**, you become an open door. Yoga's mudras automatically bring the practitioner into various states of consciousness:

> These symbolic finger, eye, and <u>body postures</u> <u>can vividly depict certain states or processes of</u> <u>consciousness.</u> Conversely, specific positions <u>can lead to the states of consciousness that they</u> <u>symbolize.</u> (pg. 2)

Another limb of the yoga tree is Tantric yoga. Yoga masters openly proclaim that the practice of Tantric yoga is occultic and magic:

> Tantric yoga is at times a bizarre but always fascinating mixture of magic, occultism, body and mind mastery, esoteric knowledge, and mysticism of cosmic dimension. (*The Complete Yoga Book*, pg. 501)

Hand signals to the gods!

Yoga masters claim that magic can meet your needs. In other words, "if you have a need for money, you call on the god of wealth, the Hindu deity named Kubera" (*Mudras: Yoga in Your Hands*, pg. 94). This calling is done by simply arranging your fingers into a specific configuration.

Through the use of mudras you are considered to "be open to the yoga." According to yoga tantrikas, "The body is now 'awakened' from its dormancy and made ready for its sacral role. To the accompaniment of mudra, it is now offered to the deity. Mudra is the ritualized body-language both of offering and of surrender. The body is depersonalized and the deity is invited to enter its pure dwelling-place" (*Kundalini: The Arousal of the Inner Energy*, pg. 31).

Satan is well acquainted with God's Word. In Genesis 1:27-30, mankind is given total dominion and authority in the earth. Therefore, the only way for Satan to accomplish his evil agenda in the earth, which is to "steal, kill, and destroy," is to oppress, possess, and invade mankind's soul and physical body.

The mechanics of mudras, mantras, and postures afford Satan legal access into the "open door" of mankind's physical body. Ignorance of these laws is no defense against Satan. The practice of yoga bombards the spirit realm with blatant pleadings and invocations to the angels of darkness.

During meditation, the yoga practitioner "often uses a mantra, a mystical holy word of power, to invoke the demon spirit guide to come" (*Dark Secrets of the New Age*, Texe Marrs pg. 114). Mantras within the occult language do much more than simply generate a vibration in the sinuses, as some yoga instructors claim:

> A mantra also serves to relax the mind into a trance state.... The concept of the mantra originated in the Hindu religion. ...the mantra which TM [transcendental meditation] assigns is invariably the name of a Hindu god. (pg. 114)

Sound vibrations are mantras of syllables that invite the essence of the "hum of the universe." According to the experts, Tantric yoga brings a maturing of the process:

> It is to the Tantras that we owe the mature development of a system of sound equations (mantra-yoga)... the sacral sound, is concerned with sound as being, i.e. with pure sonic vibration.... The Vedantic [scriptures] meditations of the Upanishads, (portion of the Vedas) continually invoke the mystic *Udgitha* (literally 'ultimate song') of the *pranava* (the basic hum of the Universe) OM [or I AM]. (*Kundalini: the Arousal of the Inner Energy*, pg. 24)

The "OM" mantra created the world, according to Kali, the mother Hindu goddess. She mocks God the Father by claiming she spoke the world into existence:

> The Mother Goddess Kali is said to have used her mantra word "om" (same as the Church Universal and Triumphant's mantra word *aum*) to create the world. (Marrs, pg. 114)

In the Hindu pantheon, Kali is fierce and dominating. She claims to liberate us from the cycle of karma, but her method of liberation is murder:

> Kali the "Black One,".... She has four arms, a third red eye and a belt made of human hands... she wears a necklace made of human skulls.... She is, in fact, the goddess of Rata (time) and is thought to end our illusions and free us from the cycle of karma by bringing us liberation from our bodies. (*The Little Book of Hindu Deities*, pg. 48)

Kali clearly gives us a picture of a demonic entity whose job is to kill human beings. Yet she is represented as a Hindu goddess who is worshipped and feared. Satan and his demons are extremely egocentric. We can see why the postures contain the names of Hindu deities. They represent themselves as Hindu gods to deceive many into worshiping them.

For example the Hindu "Universal World Soul" described as the "I am" is called the "Absolute Brahman." The complicated pantheon blurs the distinctions between the gods, so we see both Kali and Brahman responding to the "om" or "aum" utterance. In reality, the entire Hindu god chain, which is the kingdom of darkness, responds to "om."

Yoga postures speak to idols

By the utterance of this sound or simply by physical posturing of the "aum," the "Absolute Brahman" is attentive, along with all the other gods, i.e. demons. Yoga practitioners may believe they are a medium for a spirit that speaks truth, but God's Word clearly exposes the lie. Demons do not speak the truth to the medium:

> For the idols speak delusion; the diviners envision lies, and tell false dreams; they comfort in vain. (Zechariah 10:2, NKJ)

Not only is "aum," also spelled "om," spoken as a word mantra, but this resonating sound may be represented as merely a hand gesture, as described in the Shell mudra.

The Shell mudra, or "SHANKH" hand signal, is performed in the Hindu temple rituals as a religious symbol claiming to help you become "confident," "secure," and to provide you with "everything you need:"

> This mudra is used during rituals in many Hindu temples. There, the conch horn is blown in the morning to announce the opening of the temple doors. The same applies to our inner temple in which the divine light shines – it should also be opened.... Your left thumb becomes the symbol of the higher self, [Absolute Brahman Om] with which you connect yourself in love, and which lets you receive all the help you require, or which gives you confidence and a sense of security – simply everything you need. (*Mudras: Yoga in Your Hands*, pg. 76-77)

The Shell mudra manifests idols with a hand signal. These finger gestures and mantras are performed in the hope that their wishes will be magically granted.

> Now place the three fingers together, phrase your
> wish in a positive way as you say it out loud three
> times. (pg. 94)

This occult practice is another aspect of Satan's mechanics. It is clearly witchcraft, an exercise that performs incantations and postures to its gods. Witchcraft is a sin of rebellion (1 Sam. 15:23). A leading authority on comparative religion, Mircea Eliade, notes the similarities between yoga and witchcraft:

> All features associated with European witches
> are ... claimed also by Indo-Tibetan yogis and
> magicians' ... [a]long with a range of occult
> powers common to both. (*Encyclopedia of New
> Age Beliefs*, pg. 604)

> In its highest form, occult science merges
> indistinguishably with true mysticism. The heart
> of genuine occult practices is synonymous with
> aspects of the kundalini concept. Yoga and
> occult magic go hand in hand (pg. 604).

The gods of the nations are idols!

Therefore, to practice ancient rituals of yoga is dangerous physically and mentally, and the practice of yoga in all its occult forms is nothing but idol worship. According to Psalm 96:5 "the gods of the nations are idols," and in Ezekial 20:7, these idol practices are an abomination which defile us. Rather than confidence, the Shell mudra brings abomination.

Another mudra is called the "gesture of fearlessness."
The Bible tells us that the fear of God is the beginning of
wisdom, but the yoga players use witchcraft to escape the
emotion of fear. The author of *Mudras: Yoga in Your Hands*
cites an example of this "fearlessness" mudra:

> A person who frequently and fervently does the
> gesture of fearlessness, which can often be seen
> in the depiction of Indian deities, will also be
> freed from fear with time. (pg. 2)

As Christians, we are commanded to have an awesome
fear, meaning respect or reverence for God, but we know that
the common spirit of fear is not from God. We would never
use witchcraft to be set free from fear. If we become fearful,
we simply exercise our faith and believe God's Word, thereby
taking authority over the spirit of fear:

> For God has not given us a spirit of fear, but
> of power and of love and of a sound mind. (II
> Timothy 1:7, NKJ)

Unfortunately, fear rages in the unsound minds of those
who do not have faith in the One True God. Fear is a
mechanical tactic used by Satan, and to be lost in the occult
darkness is terrifying.

Shiva, the spirit of fear

As Christians, we know Satan brings fear, which is the
opposite of faith in Jesus Christ. Hinduism openly admits
the spirit of fear is a manifestation of Shiva, "the destroyer,"
the third god in the Hindu trinity: "Shiva has dozens of

manifestations in his enraged aspect, but Bhairava is Shiva at his most terrifying... [He] is especially scary since he has the power to conjure up our own worst fears... It's no surprise that his name has become synonymous with fear" (*Little Book of Hindu Deities,* pg. 30).

Strangely, the philosophies of the Hindus and Buddhists connect the spirit of fear with its gods. Another mudra, one that brings enlightenment, is called the Bhumisparsha mudra. Buddha himself is connected to the "cosmic consciousness" (aka the kingdom of Satan) by this mudra, which is also called the "gesture of enlightenment" (*Mudras: Yoga in Your Hands,* Herschi, pg. 156).

Buddha's mudra comfirms his position in the earth. Herschi explains his attempt to compare himself to Christ in the wilderness and shows that he is obliged to carry out his earthly obligations if he wants to achieve enlightenment:

> Buddha, like Jesus, was tempted by evil before he began proclaiming this teaching, but both were successful in resisting it.... Then Buddha touched the ground with the fingers of his right hand and swore he would bear witness that he was indeed quite entitled to remain on earth because of his many good deeds. (pg. 156)

There can be no comparison between Buddha and Jesus Christ. Buddha's body is dead in the grave awaiting the Day of Judgment. Jesus' body is **not** in the grave. If Satan and his army could have produced it, they would have held it up to the world. Jesus Christ was resurrected and is seated at the right hand of the Father (Heb. 12:2).

According to Herschi, Buddha claimed he is worthy because of his deeds, but man is not entitled to, nor can attain, salvation through good deeds alone. Only the shed blood of Jesus Christ can cleanse us from sin and deliver us into God's Kingdom of eternal salvation. "For by grace you have been saved through faith, and that not of yourselves; it is the gift of God, not of works lest anyone should boast" (Eph. 2:8 & 9).

You may have heard that the word "Buddha" means "the way." But we know Jesus is the Way, the only way to God. Buddha's goal is to be the way for uniting mankind with the cosmic force that practicing Buddhists and yogis consider to be Divinity.

The way to achieve this union is to perform yet another mudra, another mechanical invention of Satan, involving the closed circle of the index finger and the thumb. This mudra is the hand sign of the primary lotus posture:

> The closed circle of the index finger and the thumb depict the actual goal of Yoga – the unification of Atman, the individual soul, with Brahman the world soul. (Hirschi, pg.140)

Called the Chin mudra, the closed circle is the best known hand mudra of yoga:

> This symbolism, in particular, is the basis of the best-known mudra of yoga, the Chin Mudra. The thumb is symbolic of Cosmic (divine) and the index finger is symbolic of individual (human) consciousness. The ultimate or primary goal of yoga is the oneness of humanity with cosmic

consciousness. With this gesture, the human
being expresses this desire, this longing. (pg. 3)

Many Christians express their desire for God by the
raising of their hands during praise and worship. But our
hands can also bear crucial symbols that depict cosmic
"divine" gods.

Unsuspecting Christians on their yoga mats in the lotus
position, gesturing the Chin mudra, are signing a message
that worships cosmic gods. During the hand signaling often
they are taught to visualize their own unique symbol for the
"divine." In this way, clueless Christians are lured into occult
visualization, which projects a connection with false "divinity,"
the imitator of God:

> Imagine a symbol for the Divine (a light, triangle,
> wheel, flower or stone, etc.) It should be an
> anchor that connects you with the Divine . . .
> thy will be done. (pg. 147)

"Thy will be done?" These words echo the LORD'S Prayer.
Connecting these words to a mudra hand signal is an example
of the New Age attempt to twist language, so as to confuse,
confound, and deceive. If the goal of the mudra meditation
were to connect us to the true Divine, we would not need a
symbol. We would simply pray in faith to ask the LORD to
come into our hearts:

> "The word is near you, in your mouth and in
> your heart" (that is, the word of faith which we

preach): that if you confess with your mouth the
LORD Jesus and believe in your heart that God
has raised Him from the dead, you will be saved.
(Romans 10:8b-9)

Seek the Kingdom of God

The focus of the Christian is to seek first the Kingdom
of God and His righteousness (Matt. 6:33) and to love and
serve others. To the contrary, Satan's mechanics work in just
the opposite way. They serve him well in the mudras and
postures of yoga in prideful mystic religions that serve self
and deify the physical world:

> If we are aware that cosmic consciousness in
> all its forms manifests itself in everything and
> everyone around us, that we are connected with
> everything through our individual consciousness,
> then the first commandment of all great religions
> becomes clear to us. Love yourself and love the
> world around you – you and the world around
> you are one. (Hirschi, pg. 156-157)

New Age philosophies about love and the world are
totally contrary to what is written in the Word of God. Note
how the Scripture is reversed. "... love your neighbor as
yourself." The Bible places this command as second to loving
the LORD God:

> Jesus answered him, "The first of all
> commandments is; 'Hear, O Israel, the LORD
> our God, the LORD is one. And you shall love
> the LORD your God with all your heart, with

all your soul, with all you mind, and with all your strength.' This is the first commandment. And the second, like it, is this: 'You shall love your neighbor as yourself.' There is no other commandment greater than these." (Mark 12:29, 31, NKJ)

Note how Hirschi says to "love the world around you" and the Word of God says just the opposite.

Do not love the world or the things in the world. If anyone loves the world, the love of the Father is not in him. For all that is in the world, – the lust of the flesh, the lust of the eyes, and the pride of life – is not of the Father but is of the world. (I John 2:15&16)

The mechanics of yoga guides the practitioners to worship the world and other things that God has created until they become "one" with them. In doing so, yoga promises to show them the "path to unity:"

Simply look at an object or being (stone, plant, animal, etc). While inhaling, absorb its energy; while exhaling, give it your energy. Each breath is like a band, and the connection becomes denser and denser until you merge with it. You can connect with cosmic consciousness in this way, and it will show you the path to eternal unity. (Hirschi, pg. 156)

Are we to seek eternal unity with the creature rather than unity with the Creator? Romans 1:25 calls this perversion of the truth an abomination. Through pagan religious practices Satan hopes to trick mankind into a union with the things that are created or with demons rather than the Creator. Mankind is deceived into thinking the union is with God.

Being ignorant of true enlightenment, mankind is satisfied and surrenders to the false light. Unfortunately, Satan has taken mankind captive to do his will (II Tim. 2:26). Satan's will for mankind is that we worship the created rather than the Creator.

Each and every yoga position represents the worship of at least one god or goddess, or exalts self as God, or worships the world as God. Even the animals, the elements, and the stars and planets are worshiped through yoga rituals that are steeped in Shintoism (the worship of nature). Yoga postures, mantras and mudras have the intent to magically elevate all things that are created as equal to the Creator.

We must not take at face value the meaning of the symbols of the eastern religious leaders. They may use symbols, which appear to mimic Christian symbols, but in reality they have nothing to do with the Truth of God. Those who use these symbols in their yoga practice deny the power of God. These people have a form of godliness but deny the power of Jesus Christ, and from such people turn away! (II Tim. 3:5).

The Bible tells us that the false gods or familiar spirit guides possess powers and are sent by Satan. "The coming of the lawless one is according to the working of Satan, with all power, signs, and lying wonders, and with all unrighteous deception among those who perish..." (II Thessalonians 2:9, 10a).

The "I AM" [OM] Vibration

One sign and lying wonder of Satan is the yoga posture which directs the thoughts and enhances mental powers called Tse Mudra, meaning exercise of the three secrets.

This hand posture in combination with the humming in your head of the "vibration of the tone OM seven times" claims to bring favorable circumstances and enhances mental powers:

> Taoist monk Kim Tawm, an authority on Chinese medicine, writes: 'this mudra chases away sadness, reduces fearfulness, turns away misfortune and bad luck, and overcomes depression. It is known to increase personal magnetism and enhance the intuitive and mental powers.'(Hirschi, pg. 114)

Alluring mental powers and charisma are characteristics of the Antichrist. This same charisma is seen in yoga adepts today. They claim their psychic powers are manifested by an occult downloading process, which is nothing more than demonic transference of knowledge. This transference from Hindu deities or demons brings a sense of self-empowerment and peace within the practitioner.

Many postures and mudras represent and worship "self" and "higher self." The Atmanjali mudra #42 seduces the reader into self-hypnosis and self-delusion:

> Imagine that you are at a holy place of power...
> At holy places we feel a special energy. Try to

also feel this energy within yourself... Immerse yourself in the peace and joy of the Divine. (pg.145)

Another mudra is called the mudra of the inner self. It describes a triangle formed with body parts, including the hands and reflects the Hindu holy trinity or triune gods. "The triangle is a symbol of the Divine.... This mudra is a prayer without words – a silent meditation, a devotion to the Divine" (pg. 149).

Satan's lies and delusions are clearly being perpetrated in the above described mudra. Practitioners are worshiping gods of the Hindu trinity and are deceived to believe the gods will give them salvation, redemption, and royal rulership. But only God the Father through Jesus Christ brings salvation, redemption, and dominion. Only God supplies our needs and gives us our abilities:

> If anyone speaks, let him speak as the oracles of God. If anyone ministers, let him do it as with the ability which God supplies, that in all things God may be glorified through Jesus Christ, to whom belongs the glory and the dominion forever and ever. Amen. (I Peter 4:11, NKJ)

It is God who provides for our needs. It is God who gives us the ability to earn an income and prosper.

> And his master saw that the LORD was with him and that the LORD made all he did prosper in his hand. (Gen. 39:3, NKJ)

Jesus Christ Himself tells us how we are to abide and produce fruit:

> "I am the vine, you are the branches. He who abides in Me, and I in him, bears much fruit; for without Me you can do nothing." (John 15:5, NKJ)

But with Christ in me, I am strong and capable of anything:

> I can do all things through Christ who strengthens me. (Phil. 4:13, NKJ)

> "If you abide in Me, and My words abide in you, you will ask what you desire, and it shall be done for you." (John 15:7, NKJ)

Strength from Christ is real and anointed. Strength from yoga is a facade that shifts the source of the strength from God to your "higher self" as described in the configuration of the wheel mudra.

In Hindu writings, the "wheel of life" posture represents evolutional strategies alleging continuous reincarnations of the soul in a different flesh. This philosophy is diametrically opposed to the Christian Bible, which teaches that we die only once:

> And as it is appointed for men to die once, but after this the judgment, so Christ was offered once to bear the sins of many. (Heb. 9:27-28a, NKJ)

According to the wheel mudra, this hand sign language speaks to the "higher self" (universal soul) to evoke "godly wisdom" from within your "enlightened soul." Your enlightened soul becomes your guide:

> Visualize a figure of light, your higher self, and ask it to wisely guide you through the ups and downs of life. You can ask it anything. Then remain in silence for awhile afterward and listen – perhaps the figure of light also has something to say to you... I entrust my being to my higher self, who knows what is best for me. (Hirschi, pg. 159)

The "Angel of Light"

Nowhere in the Bible are we instructed to envision a figure of light, especially a light referred to as your "higher self," meaning Brahman, the Universal World Soul. Who do you think will show up as the "figure of light" when he is evoked through occult methods? If you said an "angel of light," you would be right. Remember, the "angel of light" is described in Scripture as Satan, and his demons are disguised as the ministers of righteousness:

> And no wonder! For Satan himself transforms himself into an angel of light. Therefore it is no great thing if his ministers also transform themselves into ministers of righteousness, whose end will be according to their works. (II Cor. 11-14 & 15, NKJ)

These "angels of light" are not gods at all, but renegade demonic spirits, the hordes of Hell, led by Satan to destroy us through the deceptive mechanics of yoga.

The ultimate snare of the devil is to deceive us into believing we have arrived into the Light, the Kingdom of God. As Christians, we are instructed in Romans 13:12, to cast off the works of darkness, and to put on the armor of light, the LORD Jesus Christ.

The major deception is that you are deluded into believing that sin does not exist and that salvation can be earned by works alone. Satan is under the delusion thinking he is perfect, so he has devised a way to delude you into thinking that you are perfect. He initiated a yoga posture using mind control to create the illusion that you can perfect yourself unto salvation. It is called the "Perfect Posture."

> Perfect Posture: *Siddhasana.* "A *Siddha* is a sage, seer, or perfected person." The extraordinary psychical faculties he has developed are called *siddhis.*" (*Complete Yoga Book*, pg. 209, fig. 83)

First of all, there is no person, with the exception of Jesus Christ, who is, in his or her flesh, "perfect" (without sin). The idea of a sinless person is the first delusion held by the yogi.

Secondly, the term *psychical* is the same word as the word psychic. By using *psychical*, the unsuspecting person might dismiss the occult connection.

Siddha also means attainment, one of the most important yogic postures. The posture directs the mind towards realization (*Kundilini, the Arousal of the Inner Energy*, pg. 107).

The yogis admit that the posture itself directs the thoughts. The posture brings enlightenment. The yogi masters have **never** denied the fact that they draw their psychic powers to realize enlightenment from their cosmic gods. The yogi has **never** denied that he willingly evokes these entities into his body acting as a medium.

If the yogis don't deny that yoga is steeped in occultism, then certainly Christians should recognize and understand that yoga is idol worship. Satan's mechanics are geared to worship idols. If you don't see that bowing to gods through yoga is evil, then pray for discernment of spirits (I Corinthians 12:10), and God will give you the eyes to see the Satanic mechanics of yoga.

Chapter

Yoga Sonic Vibrations & Sound Waves

> I trust that the Unknown, the All in All, that is
> sometimes called God, will unfold the events of
> the future that will match the vibratory frequency
> that I, and many others together, are holding and
> projecting – a sacred space where peace and
> truth prevail. (www.onyoga.com/crisis/crisis.
> *Children's Yoga: Helps Children Cope with Crisis* 4).

Yoga works on a vibratory and subliminal frequency.
Each practitioner upon his or her yoga mat unleashes sonic
vibrations that verbalize the Sanskrit alphabet through a
network of energy centers within the body, called *chakras*
(meaning wheel).

These energy centers or psychic points within the physical
body "are interlinked by numerous subtle channels known as
nadis (from the Sanskrit root nād meaning motion, vibration)"
(*Kundalini: The Arousal of the Inner Energy*, pg. 16).

While practicing yoga the activation of these wheels of
sonic vibration is automatic. No vocal utterance is necessary.
The vibrational echo of the yoga vocabulary is emitted. This
ungodly voice speaks directly to the Hindu deities singing
mystic songs of worship and evocation, summoning the
powers of the gods (pg. 24).

Numbered as seven energy centers, *chakras* and
surrounding *nadis* begin at the tailbone and move upward in

"a straight line toward the crown of the head." Its trajectory is the same path as the spinal cord in the physical body (*Total Yoga*, pg. 23). This path is taken by the serpent Kundalini coiled at the base of the spine. This Kundalini serpent is activated through yoga postures and brings different levels of enlightenment as it passes each chakra.

Each *chakra* is depicted as a lotus flower. All seven *chakras* are associated with a particular part of the body and have a corresponding sound and color that vibrates at different frequencies. The Sanskrit letters and colors on the lotus petals indicate the intensity of sound vibrations (*Kundalini: The Arousal of the Inner Energy*, pg. 39).

The *nadis* number in the thousands. There are 72,000 [sonic vibrational] *nadis*, and many of them are named. As the Kundalini serpent power rises and passes the point of each chakra, the prana (breath life/energy) "flowing through the *nadis* spins to form brightly shining circles or wheels of light" (*Total Yoga, pg.* 24). Those spinning wheels then channel the energies of the Hindu gods, i.e. demonic entities, through the physical body.

Each *chakra* is associated with one or more of the Hindu deities. Each lotus flower or *chakra* represents a specific shape and is associated with an element such as earth, wind, and fire. Each has a mantra or power word on the lotus petals (*Total Yoga*, pgs. 26, 27), "...so that with the mantra's resonance, divine power is gradually projected into the body" (*Kundalini: The Arousal of the Inner Energy*, pg. 29).

When the *chakras* and *nadis* are activated by the snake-like motion of the Kundalini, the deities are summoned, and each deity transfers a specific occult power to the yoga practitioner. The special power is called *siddhis*. "The *siddhis* associated with the Ajna *chakra*, for example, is telepathy" (*Total Yoga*, pg. 25).

According to Ajit Mookerjee, "all the sounds known throughout the Sanskrit alphabet are identified as vocables sprung from the cosmic drum of Siva, i.e. of creation itself." Siva's vocables are part of a... "sophisticated working tradition and notational system that is three to four thousand years old" (*Kundalini: The Arousal of the Inner Energy*, pg. 29). Siva, a servant of Satan, one of three gods of the Hindu trinity, claims to be the creator of the yogic alphabet.

As "creator," Siva is glorified through a series of postures which emit vowels that worship creation:

> [F]ourteen [Sanskrit] vowels gradually emerge
> from their latent condition by proceeding, with
> the Kundalini Shakti, from the Mūladhāra
> to the navel, the heart, and finally the throat
> [centres] where the first uttered sound arising is
> the aspirate, for which reason the Visarga (moon
> or Siva) is interpreted literally as 'creation...'
> (*Kundalini: The Arousal of the Inner Energy*, pg. 30)

Siva has hidden the Sanskrit alphabet deep within the yoga postures. His diabolical scheme is an incantation of witchcraft that captures the worship of the yoga practitioner. This incantation ensures that he and his demons within the kingdom of darkness have an open door to traffic with human beings. Each lotus chakra represents an ascending level of Siva consciousness.

As each lotus or chakra is pierced and activated by Siva's female counterpart, Kundalini-Shakti, that lotus chakra opens, symbolizing the activation of the vibration-frequency. The increase in numbers of the lotus petals indicates "rising energy or vibratory frequencies" of the respective chakra, each functioning as a "transformer" (pg. 39).

The more disciplined you become in yoga, the higher the Kundalini will rise and the more intense become the sonic vibrations. When Kundalini-Shakti opens the highest lotus, she and Siva are fused with the Absolute in Sahasrāra, which means Nirvana, the highest psychic center.

Vibrational channels

> According to the Trantras, to 'awaken' a mantra is to activate vibration channels and produces certain superconscious feeling-states which aid the disciple in his sādhanā [spiritual discipline]. The very sound of a mantra, or combination of mantras, has the capacity to arouse the divine forms or their energies. Each divinity possesses a bīja mantra, a seed-sound syllable, which is its equivalent. (*Kundalini: The Arousal of the Inner Energy*, pg. 29)

In other words, the mantra symbolizes a deity or cosmic force. Each syllable arouses the Hindu divine forms or their energies. These forms take on various demonic entities depending on the chakra.

Sanskrit mantra is even emitted through the basic posture called the lotus posture, which speaks a sign language that worships the Hindu trinity. Sitting cross-legged provides a stable triangle base, which sustains what is considered to be the closed circuit of the energy field. The basic energy field is the first *chakra*, which is the root <u>Muladhara chakra.</u> Here is found the "birthplace of all sounds" (pg. 30).

According to Ajit Mookerjee and Tara Fraser, the inaudible sonic vibrations being emitted are specific to each Hindu deity. For example, the base *chakra*, Muladhara Chakra, sends sonic vibrations to "Brahma and Dakin" (*Total Yoga*, pgs. 26-27).

This first *chakra* emits specific letters, which transmit five Sanskrit mantras into the atmosphere, specifically targeting the worship of planet earth (*Kundalini: The Arousal of the Inner Energy*, pg. 39).

Furthermore, there are animal deities attributed to each *chakra*. For example, the Muladhara chakra evokes Ganesha. Ganesha is an elephant worshipped and revered as the "lord of all living things" (*The Little Book of Hindu Deities*, pg. 14).

Chakra Name and Sanskrit Meaning	Deities Evoked and Worshiped	Animal Deities Represented and Worshiped	Element Worshiped	Number of Lotus Petals	Vibrational Mantras
Muladhara "Root"	"Brahma and Dakini"	Ganesha an elephant considered "Lord of all things"	Earth	Four	Five
Svadhisthana "Pelvic"	Vishnu and Rakini or Chakini Sakti	A crocodile symobol of fertility and vehicle of the god varuna	Water	Six	Seven
Manipura "Jewel City"	Rudra-the howeler The oldest manifestation of Siva	A ram - the vehicle of the fire god Agni	Fire	Ten	Eleven
Anahata "Unstruck Sound"	Ishā, Kakini-Sakti	Gazelle, the vehicle of Vayu, the Vedic god of the winds	Air	Twelve	Thirteen
Vishuddha "Purity"	Sadasiva: half Siva (male) half Sakti (female)	Airāvata a great white elephant ridden by the Vedic god Indra	Ether	Sixteen	Seventeen
Ajna "The Third Eye"	Paramāsiva: cosmic unity of Siva and Sakti	None	Supreme element	Two (large)	"OM"
Sahasrara "Thousand"	Shiva, Para-Brahma	None	Nothingness	One Thousand	Entire Sanskrit Alphabet

Note all of the illustrated *chakras*, when activated through yoga, participate in the pagan religious practice of Shintoism, the worship of the elements earth, water, fire, wind, and ether (the moon, sun, stars and planets).

The fourth *chakra*, <u>Anahata</u>, meaning unstruck sound (parā kundalini – Shakti) is the vibration of the universe, om (*Total Yoga*, pg. 27). With the transformation from the third *chakra* to this fourth *chakra*, "you are no longer master in your own house" (*Kundalini: The Arousal of the Inner Energy*, pg. 54). You have now become the "cosmic man."

At this *chakra* level the master of your house is displaced. Yoga's agenda is to take away the true master of the Christian house, Jesus Christ, and replace Him with prideful "cosmic man" enslaved to Satan. The opening of the fourth *chakra* is associated with the posture called "up facing dog" or "cobra." Both of which are representative of ungodly evil (Rev. 22:15 and 20:2).

The Bible warns of false religions, which deny the power of Jesus Christ. These false religions led by Satan will not only deceive us but will take us captive "by creeping into our household." The Bible says we will be considered gullible or easily fooled. We will claim to have a form of godliness but deny its power (2 Timothy 3:5, NKJ).

Purity brings immortality

Satan uses words like "purity" hoping to seduce us. The fifth *chakra*, <u>Vishuddha</u>, means "purity." When this *chakra* is activated, the practitioner is said to drink the nectar known as Soma, the drink of immortality (*Little Book of Hindu Deities*, pg. 84).

Ajna, the sixth *chakra*, is known as the third eye or sixth sense. It represents the Hindu "dot" as seen worn between the eyes. This vibrational energy symbolizes the inseparable Siva - Shakti, the cosmic unity whose self-luminous consciousness is all-pervading, all-transcending, and all-unifying. Mental images such as telepathy as well as abstract ideas are experienced at this level (*Kundalini: The Arousal of the Inner Energy*, pg. 44).

Sahasrara, known as Nirvana, is the seventh *chakra*. It represents the full-blossomed lotus, "self-realization." When the yogi reaches Nirvana, he has attained the highest point of transformation by the serpent Kundalini. This place is considered to be the "meeting place of the gods Shakti and Siva" (*Total Yoga*, pg. 26).

This seventh *chakra* is called "Lotus of the Thousand Petals." Here the entire Sanskrit alphabet is manifested, emitting sonic vibrations as infinite sound waves, which evoke the gods "Shiva and Para-Brahma" (pg. 26). At this highest level, the yogi is brought into unity with the Absolute World Soul (Satan). He evolves into godhood, chanting the mantra, *Om* or *Aum*. These utterances translate into English as the "I AM" through the guidance of the goddess Kundalini.

Sound waves travel without boundaries

The very thought of arousing pagan deities (demons) of eastern mystic religions is blasphemy to all of Christianity. Yet it happens. These yoga postures send out sound waves of idol worship that are timeless and that travel without boundaries throughout the universe.

The Bible tells us that we will have to answer for all the vain words we have ever spoken. "But I say to you that for every idle word men may speak, they will give an account of it in the Day of Judgment" (Matthew 12:36).

Followers of Jesus Christ would never intentionally send out sonic vibrations filled with Sanskrit mantras which worship Hindu deities. And yet, those who practice yoga are speaking words in vain and sacrificing their bodies on the yoga mat, whether they know it or not.

As Christians, we are pure in spirit and strive to be godly by taking good care of our bodies and souls. God's plan for mankind is that we stay fit and prosper. He does not want to see us in bondage to vain Hindu religious practices. These wicked practices are highly detrimental to our physical well-being and extremely dangerous to our souls.

> For bodily exercise profits a little, but godliness is profitable for all things, having promise of the life that now is and of that which is to come. (I Tim. 4:8, NKJ)

> I beseech you therefore, brethren, by the mercies of God, that you present your bodies a living sacrifice, holy, acceptable to God, which is your reasonable service. And do not be conformed to this world, but be transformed by the renewing of your mind, that you may prove what is that good and acceptable and perfect will of God. (Romans 12:1-2, NKJ)

Chapter 7

Yoga Ensnares our Children

Train up a child in the way he should go, and when he is old he will not depart from it. (Prov. 22:6, NKJ)

A spiritual battle rages in heaven for the souls of our children. They are our most precious gift from God. We must be victorious over Satan concerning the welfare of our children. Within this spiritual battle, the victor's prizes are the children. The Word of God is our weapon against Satan's evil purpose. Parents, who are nonbelievers and without the Word of God, leave themselves and their children vulnerable to the snare of the enemy.

Furthermore, there are some Christians who are saved, but Jesus is not the LORD of their lives. Consequently they send mixed messages to their children. They project the world's standards while they say they are Christians. They do not mirror their actions to reflect God's image, and thereby distort the image of God.

However, there is no time like the present to be mindful of how we reflect God's Word and His image to our children. We must be aware of the secular worldview that is taught in our classrooms. Our children spend more waking hours from Monday through Friday in school than they spend at home. Therefore, the classroom has the potential to strongly influence their lives.

God has a plan – Satan has a plot

The mind of a child is impressionable, and what he or she perceives as truth and reality is crucial. Jesus is the truth. Jesus is reality. However, Satan's ploy is to tempt our children into questioning the truth and the reality of our God. God has a powerful calling, purpose, and <u>plan</u> for each and every child. Satan, on the other hand, has a <u>plot</u> to divert our children from fulfilling God's perfect destiny. Satan can confuse the child by distorting the image of God with New Age lies in order to promote his agenda of spiritual deception.

> [T]he key manipulators of the New Age know that unless you train up and harness the spiritual direction of the children, there will be no New Age. At every level the child's worldview – that is, what he unquestioningly assumes to be true about himself and the world around him – is carefully being molded and programmed. (*Like Lambs to the Slaughter*, pg. 13)

By the spirit of Antichrist, the New Age movement encompasses the Age of Aquarius, the New World Order, and the One World religious system. Spiritual deception begins with this "One World Order," made up of a melting pot of false religious doctrines that glorify mankind as god. Unfortunately, children are seduced and indoctrinated into this evil process.

Guided imagery in the classroom

According to a 1982 New Age publication, *Holistic Living News*, there were "old souls" incarnated as children nearly three decades ago to help usher in this Age of Aquarius. Celebrating children of the New Age, the article entitled 'Guided Imagery in the Classroom' was featured on the center page, sandwiched between pictures of beautiful children practicing yoga (qt. in *Like Lambs to the Slaughter*, pg. 134).

These children are claimed to be 'old souls' who are now choosing to incarnate (possess a body) so they can help advance the Aquarius Age. One classroom teacher interviewed said that for several years he had been 'exploring' how to teach middle school children to contact their inner wisdom, to "look inside rather than outside for answers to their questions about life" (pg. 134).

More and more, the New Age Movement infiltrates our children's minds with books that teach false religious doctrine. One popular children's book entitled *Be a Frog, a Bird, or a Tree: Rachel Carr's Creative Yoga Exercises for Children*, is deceptive to the undiscerning reader. In the opening paragraphs the author portrays yoga as a benign parroting of the various insects and animals.

> Many thousands of years ago, a group of people of India invented ways to exercise based on the movements of insects and animals and birds. They discovered that if human beings could learn to move with the lightness of a frog or a bird, or to imitate shapes of bridges, wheels, and trees, and at the same time, stop and relax their muscles the way that animals do, they could become healthy and strong. So Indians began

imitating frogs, birds, bumblebees and storks....
These movements are called yoga exercises. (pg. 9)

The occult religious practice of Shintoism incorporates man's union with animals and nature. This practice and other pagan rituals are at the root of all eastern mystic religions. Hinduism and Zen Buddhism are not discussed anywhere in Carr's book. Nowhere in the book is there any mention of the dangerous occult origin or yoga's primary objective for man to be in union with their gods.

Yet, in one chapter of her book entitled, "How to Play the Game of Relaxation," Carr blatantly teaches occult visualization techniques of deep breathing and mind control in order to put the children into a trance-like state of sleep (pg. 86).

What is her point? Why does she use these techniques to teach children the basics of yoga? Carr is yet another player in New Age seduction. Our children are at risk of believing they can create their own reality. They learn to experiment with the concept of the New Age worldview rather than believe the absolute truth, the Word of God.

According to yoga theory, there is no right or wrong. Within yoga's "open arms," the New Age worldview is embraced. The game is on, and each child becomes more than a player. You are the audience, the actor, and producer. You set the stage and direct the play. Then you become your own critic. New Agers claim that all is well in the universal playground as long as you can openly and fully accept and appreciate everyone's spiritual worldview. But Christians who are following Jesus Christ are the exception and not allowed on the playground.

These New Age and eastern mystic worldviews eliminate the final authority of the holy inspired Word of God. The Word of God is not taught in the public school. The only children truly welcome in the New Age are those who will forsake the Holy Bible by turning a deaf ear and a blind eye to the Truth. Apathy and compromise toward God's Word is seeping into the minds of our children, which reflect the "politically correct" spirit of yoga's New Age face.

Certainly we Bible believing Christians cannot allow children to be turned from the Truth of God's Word. We are called to recognize any compromise of God's Word and turn our children away from sin. Satan would love for us to leave our children in the bondage of sin. But, Jesus Christ came to set the captives free (Luke 4:18). To deny that sin exists is Satan's deceitful seduction.

> If we say that we have not sinned, we make Him a
> liar, and His word is not in us. (I John 1:10, NKJ)

The universal sign of hands used in Hawaii is "you're o.k.! I'm o.k.!" The New Age religion preaches "you're ok! I'm ok!" Our children love to hear this mantra. But neither they nor their parents are OK if they are without the Word of God. Without repentance there can be no remission of sin (Luke 3:3) and without the remission of sin, there can be no salvation through Jesus Christ (Acts 2:38).

Spirit guides in the classroom

God's adversary is promoting visualization in our classrooms. One teacher led her elementary class directly into the actively demonic kingdom of Satan where the children testified they personally communicated with a voice that called himself "the babbler" and who instructed them to obey him.

> In Seattle, Washington, fourth-graders reported that the teacher had frequently asked them to lie down in a darkened room. They were then led in "relaxation" techniques in which they were asked to imagine they were made of sawdust. Then they were taught how to create a mental laboratory, where they could go anytime for counsel, healings, "instant travel".... In their laboratory, they created a "mental screen" that would help them solve any kind of problem. They were introduced to "counselors" or "guides" who would come to help them with anything they asked. These guides might be people or animals. Some of the children said that a small voice had moved inside of them called, "the Babbler," which they were told to listen to and obey. (*Like Lambs to the Slaughter*, pgs. 113-114)

"The Babbler" that moves inside of these children is none other than a familiar spirit or demon. All demons, of course, answer to Satan who through pride exalts himself against the knowledge of God. The babbler is forbidden fruit. The forbidden fruit is any high (prideful) thing that exalts itself against the knowledge of God (2 Cor. 10:4-6, NKJ).

Unfortunately, the Antichrist spirit is exalting itself throughout the world. Children are being introduced to and communicating with this spirit. Consider the consequences they will suffer. With each encounter of occult knowledge, they are pulled deeper and deeper into Satan's abyss of deceit and kingdom of darkness.

With every teacher-led experience of the "trance state," children are captured by greater strongholds and subjected to an incremental dismantling of biblical truth.

The fourth-graders continued to report what the "Babbler" taught them.

> They were taught how to wield a 'Sword of Fire,' a tool used in their 'laboratory' which they could use to draw three circles of fire around themselves – and around anything they wanted in order to bring that thing to themselves. They were taught about a 'Cord of Fire' that went up from their belly buttons or from the top of their heads and extended up into infinity which could be used to influence other people. They were encouraged to try bending spoons and rulers with their minds. They were also instructed not to tell their parents. (*Like Lambs to the Slaughter,* pg. 114)

These children are being used as Satan's tools, and God has been expelled from the classroom. There is no corporate prayer allowed in our public schools today except for a remnant who participate in student-led prayer. The restraining light of the Holy Spirit of God, once invited into our schools, is now forbidden to shine, leaving an open door to spiritual darkness.

Romans 1:24&25 describes this spiritual darkness that comes in the absence of God's light. It will cause people's "hearts to be darkened," and they will then "dishonor their bodies among themselves." As a result, promiscuity, drugs, and murder have spun out of control in the classrooms across the nation.

Witches are seducing our children

> In the "Diana Letters," in-house memos to a very large coven [of witches] in Southern California, [the witches] bragged about how many children in the area were choosing the "Pagan Way." [T]he memo emphasized, 'Each One, Reach One!' (*Like Lambs to the Slaughter* pg. 9)

With occultism increasing in the public classrooms, Christian parents can no longer afford to ignore the facts. Our children are being taught yoga meditation techniques, visualization, and guided imagery that gurus, Shamans, witches and mediums of Hinduism and Buddhism practice in their religious rituals and pagan ceremonies. On the other hand, teacher-led prayer to the Judeo-Christian God has been made illegal by laws that serve the kingdom of darkness.

In a newspaper commentary dated October 21, 2003, two men are featured sitting at a table drinking coffee discussing current day problems:

"They've taken God out of the public school, and now they want to take God out of the pledge of allegiance." [The other man replies], "And then they wonder where God is when there's a school shooting!" (The Honolulu Advertiser, Tues. October 21, 2003, pg 7A)

Politically correct schools are encouraged by administrators to express a humanist and secular point of view. Satan has accomplished this feat by using prized operatives in his covert army, the secular humanists. *Webster's New World Dictionary, Third College Edition* defines a secular humanist as a "human being who follows the 'worldly spirit' view, one who 'disregards or rejects any form of religious faith and worship.'"

When corporate prayer was removed from our schools in 1962, and yoga practice was allowed to enter, the restraining Light of God "left the building." Abraham Lincoln, in the Gettysburg Address, November 19, 1863, referred to our nation as one "under God." Certainly he would never have imagined that God would be systematically removed from the public schools of the United States of America.

The secular humanists misinterpret the meaning of our forefathers in their definition of "separation of church and state." Thomas Jefferson clearly meant to ensure that there would be no governmental interference in the people's right to worship, that the State could not dictate to religion.

Our nation was founded by Christian believers who prayed at every congressional meeting. We give sworn testimony by placing our hand on the Bible and our money declares to the world, "In God We Trust." Our nation is blessed today because we are established on the Rock of Jesus Christ.

> Blessed is the nation whose God is the LORD....
> (Psalm 33:12a, NKJ)

When our school leadership began to experience the consequences and devastation of removing prayer, they found themselves in a precarious situation. How could they re-establish order in the classrooms without seeking Godly wisdom?

In their frantic dilemma to restore order, they began opening their doors to any and all solutions. Secular humanists and the New Age movement were all too ready to offer their worldly philosophies.

Now Satan is seated in a position of power, protected by laws that allow him to seduce our children and our schools with his agenda. How ironic that secular humanists who manipulated the law to forbid prayer to the One True God now protect the teacher who leads our children into Hindu occultic trances for communion with demonic spirit guides. This outrage has been going on for years:

> In March 1982, U.S. Department of Education held seven hearings around the country on the protection of "Pupils Rights Amendment," that contained hundreds of parents' testimonies of subjection of their children to such practices as Yoga, TM (Transcendental Meditation), hypnosis, guided imagery, visualizations,

parapsychology, sensitivity training, psychiatric exercises, and other practices designed to change the thinking, values, beliefs, and behavior of the children. (*Like Lambs to the Slaughter,* pg 47)

These practices, under the satanic umbrella of mystical religions, produce union with the demonic world. Satan's overall grand scheme and solution to the problems within our schools is to restore "order" in the classrooms by zapping our children into a trance state, during which time they become "enlightened" to the One World Religion and the New World Order.

Many of Satan's loyal faculties are already in place. Many of his educators are atheists or agnostics. Many faculty members are simply clueless. But many of them are deceived and ensnared by a spirit of intellectualism. The Bible describes those who trust in their own reasoning and worldly education rather than God.

> [They are] always learning and never able to come to the knowledge of the truth. (II Timothy 3:7, NKJ)

Shakta Kaur Khalsa, a teacher of Kundilini yoga for 25 years and author of the book, *Fly Like a Butterfly,* describes how she led her Montessori classroom of children, ages 4 through 7 in visualization:

> They flexed their spines in [the] cat and cow [posture], mooing and meowing enthusiastically, stretched into Cobra, hissing all the while, balanced on their bottoms, holding their legs

up in lotus flower pose, and focused as fierce warriors in archer pose.... I guided the children in a visualization where they imagined they were lying on a warm, sandy beach.... As I looked around the room... I noticed that each of the children internalized these images in such a way that he or she relaxed more profoundly than in deep sleep. (www.childrensyoga.com pg.1, 2)

Because of the ignorance of these yoga teachers, children are being manipulated into opening themselves to the occult and becoming sacrificial offerings to demons.

Building an alter unto idols

Khalsa gives tips to her readers in order to incorporate the whole family into the yoga religious rituals, instructing them how to set up what is clearly an altar of witchcraft in their home.

If you are still not convinced that these yoga postures are religious in nature and that the practitioner bows to sacred idols of the Hindus and Buddhists, read the following quote that describes how to build an altar:

> Make a sacred space; use a small table or cover a box with a cloth. Decorate it with pictures and objects that have a special meaning for your child. Use a candle for focus during a meditative yoga time.

> Begin by closing your eyes and taking a few deep breaths. Mentally or outloud recognize the

inner guidance, and connect it to the universal guidance, however you perceive it to be. (www. childrensyoga.com pg.2)

The table is nothing less than an altar built unto the gods of the yoga rituals complete with amulets and candles commonly used in occult religious ceremonies.

Khalsa continues in her instruction to "make it child-friendly" saying, "Remember, it's better to start simply and build gradually." This direction is given so the child can receive what Khalsa calls "the great blessings from yoga."

By slowly and incrementally opening the child's mind to these occult practices, the child is less likely to become frightened or overwhelmed. Satan's objective is to seduce the child and to convince him or her to go with the flow. Satan is crafty not to alert the child to any danger.

On one website blog, a yoga teacher expresses how grateful she is for Khalsa's yoga instruction. The teacher explains that she trains children as young as 3 years old using the tools of Kundalini yoga.

Some of these children have been diagnosed with autism and ADD, yet they "are able to grasp the breathing techniques and mantras. Numerous parents have reported to me that their children use breathing and mantra to self-calm during stressful situations including waiting in lines, long car rides, and doctor visits" (www.childrensyoga.com/sharing pg. 2).

A wise man?

Furthermore, Khalsa teaches the children to "chant-up" a wise man in the Indian Sanskrit language.

> At the beginning of each class, she leads students in tuning into their inner teacher by repeating the following [Sanskrit] chant several times; *Ong namo guru dev namo (I greet the wise teacher within me and outside of me).* (www.sunandmoonstudio. com/whole.html pg 2)

The incantational chant actually invites the "wise teacher," which is a demonic spirit, into the child's very presence. As Godly parents, we must know exactly what is being taught to our children in school. We need to be able to detect any occult teaching our children might be receiving. Don't be afraid to question your child and sit in on some of the classes. These subversive indoctrinations into the occult are occurring throughout the United States to children as young as two and three years old.

Another first grade teacher led the class into a hypnotic trance technique in which the children, in an altered state of consciousness, meet another "wise man."

> In Florida, first graders listened to 'Quieting Reflex' and 'Success Imagery' tapes that took them on guided imagery fantasy trips, introduced them to the basics of yoga for the purpose of 'relaxing' the children, used powerful hypnosis techniques to help lead the children to

'significant behavior changes', and in the third tape of the series, introduced them to a 'wise man' to whom they could go for counsel. (*Like Lambs to the Slaughter*, pg. 111)

Obviously, this "wise man" is a demonic spirit seen by the children as someone who is there to help them. Within the practices of occult religions, the goal of the demonic spirit guide is to seduce the children into an esoteric relationship. This covert and "special" relationship is intended to lead them away from God's light into the kingdom of darkness, thereby potentially derailing them from their God-given destiny to enact the kingdom of God on earth.

Parents are standing up!

Many Christian teachers and parents from all over the nation are standing up against yoga religious teachings that are bombarding students with lies. They rest in the hope and truth that as Christians they are heirs of God through Jesus Christ (Gal.4:7) and have nothing to fear. They know that Christ who is in them is greater than Satan who is in the world (I John 4:4b). Our God, whose powerful Holy Spirit lives within us, always prevails over the god(s) of this world.

One schoolteacher, a committed and knowledgeable Christian, gave her testimony about a seminar she attended. The three-day seminar called a "School within a School," was designed to "help them become better teachers" by leading the children on guided imagery/visualization trips, by instructing them on how to build a psychic room, how to contact their spirit guides, how to read auras, and how to conduct out of body experiences. Fortunately, she was familiar with the occult religious nature of these activities, and she refused to participate in them (*Like Lambs to the Slaughter*, pg. 34).

One teacher at the seminar suggested that the best way to settle the classroom was simply to have the children "stand up, stretch tall, take a couple of deep breaths, and then go limp all over like a rag doll." This technique certainly would seem to relax the kids, and it manages to do so without "zapping the kids into an altered state of consciousness" (pgs. 92-93).

Unfortunately, too many teachers encourage their students to take further steps into altered states of consciousness, which is the core of all eastern mystical practices. This trance state will allow contact with the spirit guide(s) through what the yoga masters call union with the "Higher Self." In this way the student "can meet his spirit guide and experience his divinity" (pgs. 92-93). Unfortunately, their young minds are intrigued to try these new experiences.

This trance state excites the Kundalini energy, which is satanic "serpent power." Yoga adepts have warned us that once the Kundalini is awakened and if the young practitioner is not experienced in opening the doors to its power, then "the student may have difficulty closing" those doors. Therefore, any practice engaging in altered states of consciousness is especially dangerous to our children (98).

In *Like Lambs to the Slaughter*, reference is made to the book, *Meditation with Children and Meditating for Children*, an instruction manual for teachers:

> [This book] ...contains several drawings of cute and lovable snakes. [Teachers] instruct the

children to breathe in as [they] bring [their] life energy within and breathe out as [they] send [their] life energy out into the world around [them]. (pg. 97)

These "cute and loveable" snakes represent Kundalini, the serpent. Hatha yoga meditation is clearly being taught in this teacher's manual.

Eastern mysticism taught in cartoons

Teachers are not the only resource for this indoctrination into occult practices that are depicted as child's play. Our children are subjected to occult worldviews on TV and in the movies. In children's cartoons such as "Teenage Mutant Ninja Turtles" ninjas are portrayed as benign, like the loveable snake, but research reveals that real ninjas are actually killing machines. Ninjas are introduced to killing techniques at age five. Along with the art of murder, ninja girls are taught the art of seduction (*Martial Arts of the Orient*, pg. 119).

Yet our cartoon ninja turtles are portrayed as bright and colorful superheroes that order pizza and address a "rat" as a "wise man." This wise man possesses a scepter of power and openly promotes the occult belief in reincarnation.

Pokémon, a little Japanese cartoon character, embraces the martial arts traditions, like the ninja. Pokémon is full of occultic psychic powers including the art of self-transformation into various animal forms, replete with kidnapping and possessing human bodies through which he speaks.

Harry Potter is one of the most openly occultic characters

in the genre of children's literature. Harry Potter stories reek with demonic witchcraft, divination, and incantation rituals, none of which is ever defined or implied as being evil or satanic. Once we recognize what's happening in our culture with regard to subtle indoctrination, we must protest the depiction of these occult playmates who masquerade as harmless characters.

In the mid '80's, administrators attempted to force self-help methods into the minds of students as part of the curriculum. Parents in New Mexico protested the use of the "DUSO" program (developing understanding of self and others) based on the use of forty-two guided imagery and visualization fantasy stories.

Don't tell your parents!

School counselors and teachers tried to use DUSO to offer children different ways to 'relax' and to introduce them to spirit entities. According to *Like Lambs to the Slaughter,* "more than one child testified that they had been instructed by school counselors not to tell their parents" (pg. 112).

New Age doctrine is becoming more prevalent in our school systems and textbooks. Some parents have chosen to home school their children rather than submit them to these harmful indoctrinations, but the courts are making it more difficult for parents to home school.

In March, 2008, California courts ruled that home schooling parents must have a state issued teaching certificate to be able to teach their own children. We must determine to what extent we will go to protect the little ones who are so loved by Jesus (Luke 18:4, 5).

The occult New Age yoga rituals are infiltrating our communities. There are witches who claim, "The craft is really the Yoga of the West" (pgs. 319 & 320). Even the witches note that yoga is witchcraft and obtain their power from esoteric rituals.

Ancient religious rituals of yoga are intended to ensnare our children. As informed Christians, we should be able to discern any occultic practices being introduced to them. We must teach our children the weapons to defeat the adversary of God and arm them with the knowledge of the enemy's schemes.

We must show our children by example the wisdom and the power that ensues when we speak the Word of God, which is the sword of the Spirit (Ephesians 6:17b). The sword of the Spirit is our greatest weapon.

> For the weapons of our warfare are not carnal but
> mighty in God for pulling down strongholds...
> (2 Corinthians 10:4, NKJ)

We must use these weapons to fight the enemy. The enemy is not flesh and blood but principalities and powers, spiritual hosts of wickedness seated in high places, in spiritual realms (Eph. 6:12). We must protect our children from these evil powers. Our children are our greatest blessing, our most beloved gift from God. The spiritual battle rages for the souls of our children. We must never allow yoga to ensnare our children.

> Train up a child in the way he should go, and
> when he is old he will not depart from it.
> (Proverbs 22:6, NKJ)

Chapter 8

Creating Your Own Reality

Visualization and imagery practices are being pursued by millions of people around the world. New Age visualization claims to work by using the mind to influence perceptions and personal reality. Visualization also claims to uncover an inner divinity that can allegedly manipulate reality. But who or what is manipulating these illusions?

> Sir John Eccles, Nobel Prize Winner for his research on the brain, said the brain is 'a machine that a ghost can operate.' In a normal state of consciousness, one's own spirit ticks off the neurons in his brain and operates his body. We are spirits connected with a body. But in an altered state, reached under drugs, **Yoga**, hypnosis, etc., this passive but alert state, the connection between the spirit and the brain, is loosened. That allows another spirit to interpose itself, to begin to tick off the neurons in the brain, and create an entire universe of illusion. You've opened yourself up. It's called sorcery. People are literally teaching themselves how to be demonized, all in the name of developing one's full potential. (www.rapidnet.com/jbeard/bdm/psychology/yoga.htm)

"Another spirit" imposing its thoughts could indeed influence ones religious beliefs. Let's look at someone who has entered an altered state. He subjected himself to demonic influences and thereby confused prayer with a meditation that claims to create reality:

> Since September 11, I have found myself over and over again coming into a projective state of prayer, but not the kind of prayer that is asking or begging. What I am calling prayer is a practice of consciously creating reality with my vibratory energy. Anytime I forget, I just become aware again that I have the power to choose an energy projection of truth and peace prevailing on earth. (www.onyoga.com/crisis pg. 2 of 4)

The interposing spirit of the altered state conveniently and masterfully exchanges reality for fantasy, which results in implanting seeds of Hinduism where Self becomes God. The ancient Hindu prayer says:

> "Lead us from the unreal to the real, from falsehood to truth, from darkness to light." This ancient Hindu prayer expresses a core sentiment that is universal among spiritual seekers. But what is meant by "real" and "unreal"? For the yogi, only the Divine, the Self, is overwhelmingly real. All else is, if not illusory, in some way less real or unreal. (*Living Yoga*, pg. 257)

To the contrary, God is substance and reality whether you choose to believe in Him or not. He is so real that He expresses His infinite love for us by giving us Himself thereby saving us from eternal hell which is separation from Him.

We are cleansed and saved not by cosmic consciousness, postures, breathing, or false teachings about our "realized selves," but through the precious blood of Jesus Christ (John 3:16). God's plan will always triumph over Satan's plot. Those who receive Him and love Him are made one with God and set apart to rule and reign with Him.

Unfortunately the more you practice the altered state of yoga, the more the illusion of the "sacred reality" becomes truth:

> The tantric teachers were masters of ritual. They understood that the human mind could be disciplined and transcended through the repeated performance of symbolic actions. Ritual is action that is charged with symbolic significance and that connects the individual to the sacred reality. (*Living Yoga*, pg. 242)

The ancient yogic method of "creating one's own reality" is a ploy of the enemy of God to keep mankind focused away from the truth of God's Word. There is only one reality: the inerrant Word of God. To visualize and exalt a thought pattern contrary to His Word is egocentric and foolish.

Occult visualization used by yogis deludes them into perceiving themselves as "divine." In their altered state, they believe they can achieve an elevated status of being "divine" and evoke creative powers from the Kundalini Serpent, also known as the goddess Shakti. In Hindu writings, "the world is ...the playground of the goddess (Shakti)... [and they] invite the goddess, the creative spirit, into [their] lives" (pg. 242).

According to the Hindu doctrine, the union or yoking to Kundalini-Shakti can be accomplished by ritual invitation only. The yogi must do the required yogic incantation by physically posturing the body in order to facilitate the union. Practicing yoga ritual automatically opens the doors or the gates of man's soul for the indwelling of demonic spirits.

Guard your gates!

As Christians, we are to guard our gates. Only Jesus Christ should be welcomed into the gates of our soul. Only the King of Glory should be invited to dwell within us:

> Lift up your heads, O you gates! And be lifted
> up, you everlasting doors! And the King of glory
> shall come in. (Psalm 24:7, NKJ)

Unbeknown to many who create their own altered reality, they are becoming demonized. Satan and his demons know that if they can infiltrate our gates and gain control of our souls (mind, will, and emotions) then they can orchestrate events which will affect both the spirit realm and the physical realm.

Demonic enlightenment

In exchange for access into the yogi's temple (or body), the demons offer to "enlighten" the yogi to the new "sacred reality." This "reality" is the "wisdom" of Satan's corrupt viewpoint. This wisdom comes to the yogi in the form of intuition. Yogis believe that this "creative ritual of infusing the light of the spirit into [their] lives is the quintessence of all spirituality" (*Living Yoga*, pg. 242).

Yogis consider the "light" to be the knowledge of the "truth," which comes to them through "meditative intuition." In other words, yogis and eastern mystics believe that esoteric knowledge comes from self-illumination during yoga meditation. They believe that these hidden mysteries are truths revealed only to highly evolved "open-minded thinkers" such as themselves.

According to Ruth Montgomery, a New Age leader, intuition comes from spirit guides called "Walk-ins." These guides are reincarnated entities who are even now taking possession of living humans. These walk-ins are old souls from the spirit plane. In other words, your soul is invaded and oppressed by the walk-in spirit guides:

> Montgomery's cheery description of a benign process of Walk-ins taking over human bodies is in reality a horrendous picture of Satanic demons entering willing humans and bodily taking possession. Sealed by Satan, the "new" person is imbued with a reprobate mind and the New Age spirit of Antichrist. (*Dark Secrets of the New Age*, pg. 122)

These walk-ins, says Montgomery, are harbingers of a new order that brings peace on earth. Montgomery's personal spirit guides tell her that there are tens of thousands of them now in physical form. Walk-ins are New Age disciples returning at an accelerated pace to usher us into the Age of Aquarius when we will all be as one and the biblical prophecy of the millennium will be fulfilled (pg. 122).

Humans possessed by "walk-ins" and demonically enlightened yoga practitioners are New Age disciples who share a common vision of world peace on their terms. These disciples have received an occultic transference of knowledge, having been downloaded by the demonic spirits of the Hindu deities. Through intuition they obtain a new "sacred reality," one they share with other New Age disciples.

This sacred knowledge is a common vision of Satan's agenda that will incrementally prepare the way for the coming One World Order. This "sacred reality," or occult wisdom, is at enmity with God.

One mind - one "sacred reality"

Upon completion of the yoga ritual, the ancient incantation has deposited its evil "seed" into the practitioners' soul, and a newly spawned "sacred reality" is mobilized within them. The physical body is then in alignment with the mind of the demonic entity and its agenda.

These "spiritual changes" create an illusion of who we really are. Once Satan dismantles the soul he distorts reality and easily confuses the mind, will, and emotions of the yoga practitioner. By distorting God's Word, Satan successfully twists the truth into a lie (Rom. 1:25). In essence, Satan is telling mankind that the God who dwells within is really only our "Higher Self."

Satan's mantra is and always has been, "Do not look to God. Exalt your own desires and self-reasoning powers." Likewise, New Age adepts say, "Choose for yourself what is good and what is evil. Ponder everything through your Higher Self, which is the Universal Soul. The Universal Soul is connected to everything, and it enlightens you to know that you are God."

This deceitful line of reasoning is precisely what Satan used in the Garden of Eden to seduce Adam and Eve into sinning against God. Lies believed become a newly acquired "sacred reality," and the truth of God's Word becomes less meaningful, no longer absolute. Yoga is a catalyst for Satan's lies and false philosophies.

If you are doing yoga, even if it is with your church group, you are evoking the audience of Satan's demons whether you know it or not. Like a lamb brought to slaughter, you are being led to bow down in worship to God's adversaries. If you knew what you were really doing as a Christian upon your yoga mat, you would be terrified to realize that you are "giving heed to seducing spirits" (I Timothy 4:1).

Contrary to yoga teaching, the truth of God's Word does not come to the carnal mind by intuition. The Christian obtains the truth of God by revelation. *Webster's New World Dictionary, Third College Edition* definition of revelation: (1). a revealing, or disclosing, of something, a.) communication of divine truth or knowledge; specifically God's disclosure or manifestation to humanity of Himself or of His will.

As Christians, revelation and faith comes to us by hearing and recognizing God's voice through God's Word, not through an empty carnal [worldly] mind influenced by yoga rituals of New Age religion.

Revelation is the knowledge of who God is in all of His glory. We gain revelation from God as to who we are in Him. As His Kingdom children, we understand the abundance of His grace which includes the forgiveness of sin as well as the abundance of His promised inheritance (Heb. 9:15). He has given us dominion over the earth (Gen.1:26) as well as over sickness and disease (Matt. 10:1). And He has equipped us to take authority over demonic principalities and powers, which are the "spiritual hosts of wickedness" (Ephesians 6:12). To be victorious in our lives, we must obtain God's wisdom and revelation.

Chapter One of Ephesians tells us to pray for wisdom:

> [Paul prays] that the God of our LORD Jesus Christ, the Father of glory, may give to you the spirit of wisdom and revelation in the knowledge of Him, the eyes of your understanding be enlightened; that you may know what is the hope of His calling, what are the riches of the glory of His inheritance in the saints, and what is the exceeding greatness of His power toward us who believe... (Ephesians1:17-19a, NKJ)

Therefore, it is through revelation knowledge from God that followers of Jesus Christ receive wisdom, knowledge and understanding. His sheep hear and know His voice (John 10:3-4). God speaks through His prophets, and He speaks to us personally through visions and dreams:

> 'And it shall come to pass in the last days, says God, that I will pour out of My Spirit on all flesh; your sons and your daughters shall prophesy,

your young men shall see visions, your old men shall dream dreams.' (Acts 2:17, NKJ)

Revelation knowledge comes to us by the power of the Holy Spirit whom Jesus Christ calls the "Counselor" in John 14:26, John 15:26, and John 16:7 (NIV). He teaches us by revealing all that is spoken by Jesus Christ. In John 16:12-15, Jesus calls Him the Spirit of Truth:

> "I still have many things to say to you, but you cannot bear them now. However, when He, the Spirit of truth, has come, He will guide you into all truth; for He will not speak on His own authority, but whatever He hears, He will speak; and He will tell you things to come. He will glorify Me, for He will take of what is Mine and declare it to you. All things that the Father has are Mine. Therefore I said that He will take of Mine and declare it to you." (NKJ)

Everything God has, He has given to us. How will we answer the Holy Spirit regarding the practice of yoga? Each of us must choose. We can follow the Word of God and repent or refuse Godly wisdom and continue to create our own reality, turning the truth into a lie, becoming our own final authority, acting as our own god.

True followers of Jesus Christ will choose to submit to God rather than the foolish mantra of the yoga master. How will you choose?

Chapter 9

Yoga's Signs and Lying Wonders

> The coming of the lawless one is according to the working of Satan, with all power, signs, and lying wonders... (II Thessalonians 2:9)

Documented feats illustrate yoga masters sitting naked on mountaintops, melting the snow around themselves, claiming self-mastery over death and resurrection. These feats are signs and lying wonders that glorify man in his ability to produce god-like powers.

Satan and his angels use lying wonders to deceive, which are manifestations of occult magic phenomena. The longer one practices the ancient arts, the greater the vulgar displays of power become, and the deeper the demonic entanglement.

Kurt Koch, author of the book, *The Devil's Alphabet*, reveals that "as one master's yoga, the magical phenomenon increases." This increased "stage of yoga is a matter of pure demonical practices," says one yoga master "who wanted to be freed from it all." He came to Koch for help and was quite open about his lengthy training in Tibet for 10 years by a "master of magic":

> Masters of yoga who have reached the highest level of development can produce materialization, levitation, telekinesis, states of trance, the

excursion of the soul and many other spiritistic phenomena. (pg. 126)

Despite these and other warnings from ancient yogis about the dangers of yoga, Americans rush to reap the "feel-good" side effects touted by yoga enthusiasts who claim that yoga offers an extraordinary portfolio of health benefits.

A modern alternative health guide claims that "illnesses responding to yoga include asthma, backaches, arthritis, bronchitis, high blood pressure, obesity, sinusitis, nervous disorders, constipation ...and others." Dr. Norman Shealy, who has taught at Harvard University and is the founder of America Holistic Medical Association, recommended hatha yoga and the power of crystals as an essential part of natural health programs (*Encyclopedia of New Age Beliefs*, pg. 594).

These so-called "power crystals" are an occult *talisman*, any item thought to have magic power: a charm (*Webster's New World Dictionary, Third College Edition*), and are embraced by the mystic religious systems. Dr. Shealy's recommendation of the use of crystals is contradictory to biblical healing methods. Most of what yoga claims regarding physical healing is not physical healing at all, but it is the eradication of psychosomatic ailments through meditations of the postures, which lead to change in social behavior and personality:

It is in the field of psychosomatic ailments that yoga therapy can be most effective. ... Eventually, yoga leads them to meditation hence to modifications of personal and social behavior. (*Encyclopedia of New Age Beliefs*, pg. 594)

Yoga is still a fairly new phenomenon in America, although the yoga masters are well past the embryonic stages of the "feel good health craze." The swamis of yoga do not boast exercise and good health as their primary benefits, but instead their "claim to fame," according to the most advanced gurus, boasts the performances of "great and mighty feats." These masters performing signs and lying wonders have risen from perdition like the emerging demonic frogs coming out of the dragon as described in Revelation:

> And I saw three unclean spirits like frogs coming
> out of the mouth of the dragon, out of the mouth
> of the beast, and out of the mouth of the false
> prophet. For they are the spirits of demons,
> performing signs, which go out to the kings of
> the earth and of the whole world, to gather them
> to the battle of that great day of God Almighty.
> (Rev. 16:13-14, NKJ)

The dragon is a picture of Satan (Rev. 12:9), the beast a picture of the Antichrist (Rev. 13:11-18), and the false prophet echoes the New Age yoga voice, which sets the stage for the ushering in of the Antichrist union with man. The yoga adepts perform great signs and lying wonders in order to seduce people into following in the footsteps of their occultic rituals.

The major players and perfected yogis do not consider yoga to be just another benign exercise for the union of one individual's spirit, soul, and body. The union that yogis want to achieve is between man and his Hindu deities, i.e. antichrist spirits. Thus the performance within the physical body is extremely powerful and beyond human capability.

These superhuman powers bring glorification to man and idols, not to God.

According to the yogi gurus, the power lies in the manipulation of the breath within man, which produces phenomenal signs and wonders. The Chi is a Chinese term which means "air or breath."

> Chi gives the user "phenomenal strength," and "bequeaths to its practitioners good health, sound blood circulation, and a youthful appearance" and ... "at any given moment, directs this invisible energy to any part of his body." (*Martial Arts of the Orient*, pg. 50)

The "Chi" is summoned by the practitioner and brings with it the so-called "serpent power" that lies dormant at the base of the human spine. This "serpent power," called the Kundalini, travels upward through the seven energy centers or chakras of the body until it reaches the mind. When it hits the brain, it brings with it "enlightenment" of the esoteric mysteries.

Yogic methods to mystify

It is through this occult power that the extraordinary feats are mastered. These extraordinary feats, according to *The Complete Yoga Book*, are dependent on the successes of the yogis to have "advanced skill in pranayama [breath control] and tumo" [engendering body heat] (pg. 130).

Even Houdini bowed to the Hindu gods by using yogic methods to mystify his audience. In 1926, Harry Houdini, one of the most famous escape artists, broke the rule of silence regarding the esoteric secrets of his magic.

> [H]e revealed the secret of one of his most mystifying performances... Houdini used to survive 1 ½ hours in a sealed iron coffin at the bottom of the swimming pool of New York's Shelton Hotel.... [He used] the method of swallowing and regurgitation [of air]... a Yogic method of bodily mastery. (*pg. 130*)

Harry Houdini earned the title of magician through occult magic. The title of "magician" is defined in *Webster's New World Dictionary, Third College Edition,* as "an expert in magic; ... a sorcerer; wizard." The Word of God clearly forbids such practices:

> "There shall not be found among you anyone who makes his son or his daughter pass through the fire [human sacrifice], or one who practices witchcraft [divination], or a soothsayer [telling of the future], or one who interprets omens, or a sorcerer, or one who conjures spells [witch], or a medium [intermediate or psychic], or a spiritist, or one who calls up the dead [necromancer]. For all who do these things are an abomination to the LORD, and because of these abominations, the LORD your God drives them out from before you." (Deut. 18:10-12, NKJ)

An even greater feat of magic is recorded using the technique of burial and resurrection displayed on many occasions by yogis in India. This feat involves going into a "trance state" to simulate death:

> Resurrection of the 'dead' is a fairly common exercise in Indian magic. I have seen it done twice. The adept undergoes twenty-four hours of secret preparation, which consists in purgation, fasting, and 'swallowing' air.
>
> Before the trance state is induced, the adept is in a state of oxygen intoxication. Then, pressing his carotid arteries, he passes into unconsciousness. His disciples bury him. ...the adept remained thus [in the death trance] for an hour.... Doctors who examined the 'corpse' stated that there was no sign of life. When the given time had elapsed, the adept came to life. (*The Complete Yoga Book,* pg. 131)

Satan, the imitator of God, wants to deceive mankind by attempting to operate within the same marvelous power of signs and wonders as God. It is written, however, that God numbers our days and our steps on this earth (Job 14:5 & 16). It is by Jesus' work on the cross that Satan is defeated and has no real power over death. Only through the sin of man becoming a medium can the demons imitate death and resurrection.

The sin of witchcraft and magic are forbidden practices for the children of God because magic seeks and apprehends demonic powers. There are, of course, benign tricks and demonstrations, such as "pulling a rabbit out of a hat" or sleight of hand card tricks, that do not incorporate occult magic. What is demonstrated in ancient yogic methods of occult magic goes well beyond sleight of hand tricks. Yogic ritual draws its power from demonic sources.

Second Thessalonians 2:5-10 reveals that Satan gives his power to the "lawless one" who is to come. The Antichrist, called the beast in Revelation, may likely use the yogic methods of death and resurrection to seduce the nations into following his signs and lying wonders:

> And I saw one of his heads as if it had been mortally wounded, and his deadly wound was healed. And all the world marveled and followed the beast [the Antichrist]. (Rev. 13:3, NKJ)

The Bible tells us that men follow the beast of Revelation because Satan, operating through a man called the Antichrist, is able to replicate death and resurrection. Many will be deceived into following the beast.

Among the numerously deceived people are those who believe and accept the signs and lying wonders rather than the truth of God. The Bible describes the condition of all of us who were once under the influence of the spirit of Satan:

> And you He made alive, who were dead in trespasses and sins, in which you once walked according to the course of this world, according to the prince of the power of the air, the spirit who now works in the sons of disobedience, among whom also we all once conducted ourselves in the lusts of our flesh, fulfilling the desires of the flesh and of the mind... (Eph. 2: 1-3a, NKJ)

Yoga gone bad!

However, Christians made alive in Christ, commit spiritual adultery when practicing yoga. By voluntarily re-opening the door to Satan's spiritual realm, we subject ourselves to demonic mental and physical abuse. Documented cases of insanity and death are evidence of yoga's dangerous effects. Many advocates of yoga warn of the serious consequences:

> [T]he practice of yoga can mean death or insanity. Practitioners of yoga often warn of the power of the kundalini energy, represented as a serpent coiled at the base of the spine. . . . [T]he yogis themselves caution that this is no child's play. One might get burned (literally!) by the serpent's hot breath – or go insane. (*Confronting the New Age*, pg.77, 78)

The awakened Kundalini serpent can be a horribly violent and sickening experience:

> [W]hen describing the "awakening of the Serpent Power (Kundalini)," which they say "can be accompanied by dramatic physical and psychological manifestations called kriyas," which include "powerful sensations of heat and energy streaming up the spine, associated with tremors, spasms, violent shaking, and complex twisting movements." They also mention "involuntary laughing or crying, chanting of mantras or songs,... emitting of vocal noises and animal sounds, and assuming spontaneous yoga gestures (mudras) and postures (asanas)."

Other physical manifestations include "nausea, diarrhea or constipation, anal or uterine contractions, clenching of the jaws, rise and drop of temperature, and bulimia or loss of appetite. The entire body can be rigid or limp, and feel unusually large or small." (pg. 78)

In spite of these frightening symptoms of "yoga gone bad," the yogis claim positive beneficial side effects of awakening the Kundalini, but not without a cost:

> [In addition to]... "ecstasy, orgasmic raptures, and states of indescribable peace and tranquility," one must risk a total breakdown (or worse) for that prize. (pg. 79)

Many yoga gurus openly admit they become glorified by "awakening the serpent power." From a 1995 UN Women's Conference in Beijing, China, the New Age speaker Shri Mataji explains the awakening of the serpent power, Kundalini:

> The one thing you must note is that the awakening of the Kundalini and thus achieving self-realization is a living process of evolution for which we cannot pay anything.... When this Kundalini rises it connects you to the all pervading power, which is vital and which is an ocean of knowledge as well as an ocean of bliss.... Many diseases, even some incurable ones have been cured by the awakening of the Kundalini.... [Once] you have achieved your self-realization, you have attained all the powers that can be utilized. You become very powerful...

and at the same time you understand that you are now glorified. (www.sahajayoga.org/QuotesAndTalks/Beiging.html, pgs. 4-6)

A "medium" performance

Another example of following deceiving spirits for physical healing without regard to God's Word was seen on ABC *Prime Time Live*, February 10, 2005. The "master" over the deceiving spirits called himself "John of God" and was a farmer by trade who acted as a medium for the spirits of the deceased.

It was reported that thousands lined up wearing white clothing, a prerequisite of John of God, to receive their healings. He claimed, "...It is not me who performs these surgical procedures but one of the many spirit surgeons through me, some of which are dead."

In fact, he claimed he couldn't even remember performing such feats and that he must have been sleeping when the spirits took over his body. He was astonished and felt queasy as the interviewer began showing him some of the pictures of the bloody procedures he had performed. Surprisingly, all procedures were done without knives or anesthesia.

Born in 1942 in Brazil, John of God claims he was "first visited by King Solomon." The televised session began with all holding hands in a circle. John then instructed them to "pray to the gods."

During the course of the invocation of the gods, John of God began to show manifestations of demonic possession, or according to him, one of the "great spirit surgeons" entered his body. John of God treated several of the sick by forcing a piece of gauze held by stainless steel forceps up one of their nostrils. Once the gauze was shoved up as far as it could go, John of God twisted the forceps in a circular motion two or three turns until blood splattered down the front of their white clothing. While this made the audience cringe to watch what appeared to be an extremely painful experience, the patients claimed they had limited discomfort.

Aired on the same program, another surgical exploit included psychic surgery. This occultic practice is common in yogic and voodoo circles but always seems to provide a shocking and vulgar display of demonic signs and lying wonders. John of God proceeded to awe the audience as he created a gaping hole in a woman's abdomen using only his fingers.

The results of their healings were not nearly as dramatic as the show put on by John of God and his familiar spirits possessing his body. Out of the six cases followed in the documentary, only one man seemed to surprise his doctor when they saw marked reduction in the size of his brain tumor. One other woman who was diagnosed with chronic fatigue syndrome also claimed she felt a little better. However, the others saw no improvement. The Prime Time Interviewer had a shoulder problem and was also treated by John of God and claimed no improvement.

Engaging the "tumo"

Let's look at one of yoga's occult sources called the power of "tumo." Tumo is defined in *The Complete Yoga Book* as "the technique of engendering body heat at will":

Mme Alexandra David-Neel.... In her book *With Mystics and Magicians in Tibet*, (pg. 113) she calls *tumo* "the art of warming oneself without fire up in the snows." This art enables hermit Yogians to spend the winter in snow-girt caves at altitudes between 11,000 and 18,000 feet, wearing only a single thin cotton garment, or even no clothing at all. (pg. 134)

Evoking the "tumo" through ritualistic breath controls and various yoga postures is a by-product of occult magic. Engaging the "tumo" automatically summons "demonic" powers, which performs signs and lying wonders. In exchange for the practitioner's invitation, the demonic entity inhabits the practitioner's physical body and demonstrates great feats of magic.

Manifested occultic powers

These feats of magic are not revealed or even discussed within the westernized yoga class. Yet through yoga meditations, these signs and lying wonders are awaiting their time to be manifested as occultic powers.

Peter Lewis, the author of *Martial Arts of the Orient*, describes "Chi" (energy of the breath) as some kind of superpower entity that can protect man's body from injury simply by controlling the mind. Great concentration is required in order to develop this chi energy.

It has been said that masters in ancient China could summon their chi so quickly and direct it to any part of the body, that if they were attacked with a bladed weapon, the blade would not be able to penetrate the skin. (pg. 50)

Likewise, when Satan manifests "tumo" (warmth in the body), the guru's testimony is replete with claims of self-induced healing, self-induced purification and self-salvation (pg. 40).

Lewis also cites the following:

> A master of chi-gung... has held his hands palms uppermost and within minutes his hands have began to radiate heat – not just warmth but real heat.... A member of the audience has attempted to cut through a chi-gung master's skin with a cleaver, but after five minutes or so, after making no impression, has given up. (pg. 50)

Another account was a case of a slim young woman lying on her back and allowing a 200 pound man to jump off a table onto her stomach. She suffered no harm as she resisted the impact by directing her chi to that area.

The signs and lying wonders continue with yet another egocentric and vain demonstration of occult power: a small bed of nails was placed, sharp ends down on a practitioner's stomach, while he lay on his back. Seven bricks were stacked on top of the bed of nails. A student of the swami then proceeded to pound the bricks with a hammer until every one of them was broken. The master then removed the bed of nails from his stomach, clearing away the debris and showed that there was not a mark on him, not even the slightest indentation (pg. 50).

To conjure up or summon these occult powers exalts one's imagination against the knowledge of God and apprehends sorcery and magic. The adept opens himself to "unclean spirits" (Matthew 12:45, Mark 5:8-20) who are then unleashed to perform signs and lying wonders:

> "For false Christs and false prophets will arise, and they will show great signs and wonders, so as to deceive and lead astray, if possible, even the elect." (Matt. 24:24, Amp.)

A yoga induced transformation

As we continue looking at the devastating effects of yoga, keep in mind that these are people who are being entrapped in the web of deception. Such was the case for Christina Grof, who was an average housewife and through the practice of yoga was brought into New Age leadership:

> She took up yoga entirely without suspicion as a practice that would help her physically during her pregnancy. After all, there are widespread claims that "during pregnancy, yoga exercises are extremely beneficial and will keep you supple and relaxed." However, Grof got far more than she had bargained for, she was transformed from a "conservative suburban housewife" into a New Age leader by means of hatha yoga. All she had to do was "join a hatha yoga class for exercise" and the logical progression ensued. (*Encyclopedia of New Age Beliefs*, pg. 597)

Christina's experience with hatha yoga introduced her first to a guru and then to the serpent:

> During the birth of my first child, for which I had prepared with the Lamaze method of breathing (very much like yogic *pranayana*) this enormous spiritual force was released in me. Of course, I didn't understand it and was given morphine to stop it as soon as the baby was born. . . Then the same thing happened when my second child was born. This all lead to more and more experiences. I threw myself into yoga, although still not acknowledging it as a spiritual tool. My meeting with Swami Muktananda really blew the lid off everything. He served as a catalyst to awaken what I had been resisting, which was kundalini (the universal life force). (pg. 597)

Yoga was practiced by Christina as an innocent exercise. Yet, this occult force, or demonic spirit, led her to numerous psychic experiences that dramatically changed her life. She became a disciple of the Hindu guru Muktananda and later assisted other people in "spiritual emergencies."

At one point, she paid a price mentally as she delved further into yoga:

> Initially, however, as the standard kundalini yoga symptoms emerged in her life, the prognosis was not good... Grof herself was in the midst of a spiritual emergency and increasingly convinced of her own insanity. 'I was convinced I was

headed for a life of psychopathology. I was afraid
I was going crazy.'(pg. 597)

Then under the advice of occult counseling, Grof began
taking hallucinogenic drugs:

> Nevertheless, counseling through occult
> philosophy put matters in their "proper"
> perspective. Her marriage ended... and the late
> popular mythologist Joseph Campbell [guru]
> helped her recognize, 'The schizophrenic is
> drowning in the same waters in which the mystic
> is swimming with delight'. He also referred
> her to LSD and consciousness researcher [and
> future new husband] Stan Grof for continued
> counseling. (pg. 597)

The next chapter of her life is fulfilled by creating her
own reality, which she confuses with "blissful" insanity:

> The rest is history... and today [they] coordinate
> some 50 SEN (Spiritual Emergency Network)
> regional information centers around the globe....
> A chapter in a recent book edited by Stan and
> Christina Grof, *Spiritual Emergency*, reveals a basic
> approach of SEN counseling. The title is "When
> Insanity is a Blessing."(pgs. 597-598)

Ultimately, the insanity with which she is "blessed" grows
into full-blown occultism:

> Thus a slow but sure yoga-induced occult
> transformation catapulted Christina Grof head

long into the world of occultism.... In the long run, her innocent flirtation with yoga altered her entire life and resulted in her becoming a leader in the New Age movement, with influence over hundreds of thousands of people. (pg. 598)

Grof's innocent flirtation brought her under the influence of demons. Yoga philosophies and practices are "doctrines of demons" because they are contrary to the Word of God:

> Now the Spirit expressly says that in latter times some will depart from the faith, giving heed to deceiving spirits and doctrines of demons, speaking lies and hypocrisy, having their own conscience seared with a hot iron, forbidding to marry, and commanding to abstain from foods which God created to be received with thanksgiving by those who believe and know the truth. (I Tim. 4:1, NKJ)

Test the spirits! Are they of God?

Unfortunately, these abominable practices have become commonplace in America. Now, more than ever, millions of people are entrusting their very lives to the "doctrines of demons," giving heed to seducing spirits through the New Age religious voice.

Like an iceberg lurking below the surface, potentially destroying massive ships upon collision, so are the hidden incantations of yoga and other New Age deceptions. These signs and lying wonders are ready to bring destruction to the unsuspecting practitioner. God warns of these wicked spirits:

> Beloved, do not believe every spirit, but test the spirits, whether they are of God; because many false prophets have gone out into the world. By this you know the Spirit of God: every spirit that confesses that Jesus Christ has come in the flesh is of God, and every spirit that does not confess that Jesus Christ has come in the flesh is not of God. And this is the spirit of the Antichrist, which you have heard was coming and is now already in the world. (I John 4:1-3, NKJ)

God's Word calls us to repent from practicing the ancient arts of yoga that transform the practitioner into a medium. As we see signs of the "latter times," we continue to see evil increase. More and more Christians are flocking to all sorts of false doctrines. Nonetheless, we are called to put away our idols:

> Moreover Josiah put away those who consulted mediums and spiritists, the household gods and idols, all the abominations that were seen in the land of Judah and in Jerusalem, that he might perform the words of the law which were written in the book that Hilkiah the priest found in the house of the LORD. (II Kings 23:24, NKJ)

Hilkiah, the priest referred to here, is likened unto Hezekiah who walked in the ways of his ancestor David. Hezekiah was the first Judean king to remove the sacred poles, pillars, and the bronze serpent used in occultic rituals (II Kings 18:4).

We too, must tear down the "high places" where the gods set themselves up to be worshiped. As Christians, we are born again into the Kingdom of God and should be followers of Jesus Christ. According to Revelation 1:6, we are kings and priests. Therefore, let us desire the same heart as David, Hezekiah, and all the faithful kings and priests who have gone before us. Let us do what is right in the sight of our Father God.

Let's bring Satan and his demons down from their exalted places. We have been given authority over the unclean spirits to cast them out (Matthew 10:1). No more should we be deceived into worshiping these impostors who claim to give us wisdom, harmony, and peace through their occult rituals.

There is only one Prince of Peace. "For there is one God and one Mediator between God and men, the Man Christ Jesus, who gave Himself a ransom for all..." (I Timothy 2:5, 6a). He makes intercession for us always! (Rom. 8:34 and Heb. 7:25).

> Therefore take up the whole armor of God, that you may be able to withstand in the evil day, and having done all, to stand. Stand therefore, having girded your waist with truth, having put on the breastplate of righteousness, and having shod your feet with the preparation of the gospel of peace; above all, taking the shield of faith with which you will be able to quench all the fiery darts of the wicked one. And take the helmet of salvation, and the sword of the Spirit, which is the word of God; praying always with all prayer and supplication in the Spirit.... (Eph. 6:13-18a, NKJ)

Don't be deceived by signs and lying wonders! Fight the good fight of faith (I Tim. 6:12). We are victorious in Jesus Christ! Walk in the fullness of God's blessings, experience God's miracles, and witness His marvelous signs and wonders!

Chapter 10

Poses That Kill
...Prayers Bring Life

Yoga's aim is to separate its practitioners from God spiritually and bring physical death. All types of yoga have latent abilities to arouse the Kundalini (serpent power) and these **poses can kill** both spiritually and physically. Throughout this chapter, we will examine specific spiritual and physical characteristics of yoga. Several testimonies will clearly expose yoga rituals as demonic, not divine.

Yet, because of the lack of knowledge regarding yoga's dangers, there has been a growth explosion of make-shift yoga classes. Both novice yoga instructors and practitioners believe they are simply involved in an exercise class. They have not done any research on the mantras spoken in the Sanskrit language of the Eastern Indians; much less do they understand the spiritual worship steeped in the choreographed sequencing of the postures themselves. As a result, reports of physical, mental, and spiritual disorders are pouring in.

For example, one incident centers on a female patient with an adrenal malfunction. New Age yoga educator Richard Kieninger cites it was the lack of education on the part of the yoga practitioner and her physician which left her untreated and proved to be fatal:

A woman of my acquaintance upset her hormonal balances doing this yoga exercise, and it produced a malfunction in her adrenal glands. Doctors didn't know how to reverse the effects....and she soon died. (*Encyclopedia of New Age Beliefs*, pg. 604)

Risks and hazards of yoga

Citations taken from authoritative texts describe the risks and hazards of performing the ancient occult rituals. Warnings range from slight, almost undetectable adverse effects such as fever and blood disorders, to insanity or death. These effects are claimed to be caused by the physically erratic or withheld breath during performance of the postures. Swamis warn that advanced forms of patterned breathing within common yoga exercise, can cause a person to harm themselves irreparably.

Swami Purohit advocates a strong understanding of yoga practice before going into the postures. He claims that permanent damage, which occurs during these exercises, cannot be organically explained by doctors:

[U]nless the foundation is firmly laid, they should not practice postures and breathing exercises. In India and Europe, I came across some three hundred people who suffered permanently from wrong practices; the doctors on examination found nothing organically wrong and consequently could not treat or prescribe. (pg. 604)

Because of the nature of the various disorders, most medical doctors, unfortunately, do not consider yoga as a possible cause or link. Yet, authoritative texts by Sir John Woodroffe lists very specific complaints of considerable pain, physical disorder, and even disease, and "Hans Ulrich Rieker lists cancer of the throat, all sorts of ailments, blackouts, strange trance states, or insanity" [can result] (pg. 605).

Other specific mental and physical consequences stemming from practicing the ancient ritual of yoga are listed including blood disorders, disease, and even madness. Many people have brought upon themselves incurable illness or insanity by neglecting hatha yoga prerequisites, and by any mistake, there arises cough, asthma, head, eye and ear pains, and many other diseases. Other warnings come from Swami Prabhavananda in his book *Yoga and Mysticism* (qt. in *Encyclopedia of New Age Beliefs*):

> Now we come to breathing exercises. Let me caution you; they can be very dangerous. Unless properly done, there is a good chance of injuring the brain. And those who practice such breathing without proper supervision can suffer a disease which no known science or doctor can cure. It is impossible, even for a medical person, to diagnose such an illness....[for example], I had known a young boy of perhaps 16 or 17 years of age who had begun to practice Hatha Yoga.
>
> [H]e was acting very strangely. He would prostrate fully on the ground, rise to full height, then repeat the performance - over and over again. The Swami said that he had lost his mind...

Finally, however, he became so unmanageable
that he had to be confined.... yet Vivekenanda,
Ramakrishna's disciple, encouraged [hatha yoga].
(pgs. 605, 606)

Spiritual advisor warns of yoga's dangers!

The same kinds of warning regarding Hatha Yoga [breath
control or union of the breath] comes from United Nations
spiritual advisor and spiritist Sri Chinmoy, author of *Yoga
and the Spiritual Life*:

> ...To practice pranayama [breath control] without
> real guidance is very dangerous. I know of three
> persons who have died from it. (*Encyclopedia of
> New Age Beliefs*, pg. 604)

Another standard authority on yoga explains other
drastic effects:

> Gopi Krishna warns of possible dangers of such
> yoga practice including "drastic effects" on the
> central nervous system and the possibility of
> death.... *The Hatha Yoga Pradipika* (Chapter
> 2, vs. 15), warns, 'Just as lions, elephants and
> tigers are tamed, so the prana, [breath] should
> be kept under control. Otherwise it can kill the
> practitioner.' (pg. 605)

While Hatha Yoga is one way to induce altered states
of consciousness, all forms of yoga are intertwined and one
cannot be separated from the other or performed without
detrimental affects upon the practitioner. In the Hindu

scriptures, the *Bhagavad-Gita*, yoga practiced on a superficial level is acknowledged as potentially dangerous:

> Thus, Hindu master Sri Krishna Prem cautions in *The Yoga of the Bhagavad-Gita*, "As stated before, nothing but dangerous, mediumistic psychism or neurotic disassociations of personality can result from the practice of [yoga] meditation ..." He warns, "To practice it, as many do, out of curiosity... is a mistake which is punished with futility, neurosis, or worse ('even insanity itself')." (602:XV, 406) (*Encyclopedia of New Age Beliefs*, pg. 605)

Yoga gurus consider these hazards to be due primarily to "wrong breathing" practices while performing the postures. While yoga can produce an overproduction of nitric oxide gas, the primary hazards exist because of the "union" with the demonic powers latent within the postures themselves.

The by-product of yoga is the insidious display of satanic power brought on by the awakening of the Kundalini to bring occult enlightenment. Yoga is now practiced by millions of Americans, including professing Christians in mainline churches.

The title of this chapter, *Poses that Kill*, may seem to be somewhat an overstatement but make no mistake about it, the Kundalini serpent nature and primary objective is to spiritually kill the soul of the yoga practitioner:

> As yoga authorities Feuerstein and Miller comment, yoga results in a progressive

dismantling of human personality ending in a complete abolition. With every step (anga) of Yoga, what we call "man" is demolished a little more. (pg. 600)

Documented sources describe the impact of the Kundalini arousal which clearly results in the dismantling of the human mind. Testimonies of temporary and permanent states of insanity are documented, with radical changes in the physical body including manifestations of schizophrenia and possession of the practitioner by a demon spirit. Kundalini arousal is not restricted to Hatha Yoga practice as commonly thought. Yoga authorities say that all yoga is ultimately Kundalini Yoga, and yoga is meaningless without it (pg. 606).

Hot currents of the Kundalini

Yoga authority, Hans Rieker, concurs with this conclusion. "Kundalini [is] the mainstay of all yoga practices..." (pg. 606). He warns in his book, *The Yoga of Light*, "if the breath is prematurely exhausted [withdrawn] there is immediate danger of death for the yogi" (qt. in *Encyclopedia of New Age Beliefs*, pg. 605).

The hazardous physical manifestation of the Kundalini Shakti is described by yoga advocate, Swami Narayanananda from his writings, *The Primal Power in Man or the Kundalini Shakti*:

> These hot currents that reach the brain center heat the brain, make the mind fickle, bring insomnia, brain disorder, insanity and incurable diseases. For the hot currents keep the mind

wide awake and if a person does not know how to check the currents and to bring down the partly risen kundalini shakti to safer centers, one suffers terribly and it may ruin the whole life of a person or lead to insanity. This is why we see many become insane, many get brain defects, and many others get some incurable diseases after deep sorrow.

(qt. in *Encyclopedia of New Age Beliefs*, pg. 607)

The following example describes how a seemingly innocent yoga practice affected a woman named Carole:

Carole was very sick and doctors were unable to find the cause of her illness. When she went to a physician-nutritionist recommended by a friend, she found some literature in his office about the Himalayan Institute... Carole decided to attend the institute, where she began lessons in hatha yoga. Eventually, she was initiated and received her mantra, or word of occult power, from Swami Rama. As he laid his hands upon her head, the typical transfer of "occult energy" began, (termed Shatipat diksha). Carole was in heaven:

'Currents of electrical energy began to permeate my head and went down into my body....It was as if a spell had come over me, the bliss that I felt was as if I had been touched by God. The power that had come from his hand, and simply being in his presence, drew me to him irresistibly.'

The night after receiving her mantra, Carole was visited by a spirit being who claimed to be the spirit of Swami Rama himself. Although no one had ever mentioned the spirit world in her church (they did not believe in such things), Carole felt that this was the means of directly communing with God...

... 'almost entrancing thoughts were impressed into my mind, "meditate, meditate, I want to speak with you." It was a miracle, I was communicating with the spirit world. I had found God. Sitting in the darkness of my living room, I began to repeat my mantra. A presence seemed to fill the room. I began to see visions of being one with the universe and the magnetic thoughts were now leaving and I was hearing a voice, which identified itself as Swami Rama, saying he was communicating with me through astral travel.

Within one week, after meditating many hours each day and still in constant communication with this spirit, forces began to come upon me and gave me power to do yoga postures; I was floating through them, the forces giving me added breath even... postures that before would be very painful to do.' (*Encyclopedia of New Age Beliefs*, pg. 598)

The story continues to explain that after two weeks of meditation, "voices that once claimed they were angelic turned threatening, even demonic. ... She was brutally assaulted, both physically and spiritually by spirits." She agonized with the spirit to leave her. Then her mother took her to the Unity School of Christianity to enlist her "psychic" friend's help.

Unity Church beliefs are described in a pamphlet by Keith L. Brooks. Note the parallels of the doctrines of the Unity Church to the religions of eastern mysticism:

> Regarding Jesus Christ: Unity says.... The Krishna of the Hindu is the same as the Christos of the Greeks and the Messiah of the Hebrews... This Christ or perfect man idea existing eternally in divine mind is the true spiritual, higher self of every individual. [As far as redemption and salvation, Unity states]... The error lies in the belief that He [Jesus Christ] was the Only begotten Son of God, and that He overcame for us, and that by simply believing on Him we are saved. (*Comparing Christianity with the Cults*)

Contrary to the beliefs of the Unity Church, God's Word declares in John 3:16 that Jesus Christ is the only begotten Son of the Father and "that whosoever believes in Him shall not perish but have everlasting life." Many New Age churches today have a form of godliness but deny the power of Jesus Christ. We are instructed to leave or turn away from this apostate teaching (II Timothy 3:5).

Not surprisingly, Carole's mother's friends from the Unity Church were unable to deliver her from demonic spiritual possession:

> The psychic friends from a local church of the Unity School of Christianity... laid hands

on Carole and commanded that the "divinity within" deliver her, but to no avail. (*Encyclopedia of New Age Beliefs*, pg. 599)

The Bible clearly states that Satan will never cast out Satan. In Mark 3:23, Jesus explains that this kind of division of Satan's evil forces would bring an end to Satan's kingdom.

Remember, Carole is oppressed and possessed by a demonic spirit. The demonic spirit would not leave Carole by the authority of another demonic spirit. The psychic friends are mediums. Mediums employ demonic spirits in order to perform their signs and lying wonders. Satan will never rise up against himself; likewise, one demonic spirit will never cast out another demonic spirit. It is only by the power of the name of Jesus Christ that demons are cast out (Mark 16:17).

In and out of mental hospitals

Carole continued on the wrong path in her frantic search to be delivered. In and out of mental hospitals, being treated by New Age doctors, Carole was then referred to a spiritist:

> Dr. C. Norman Shealy, MD, PhD... a noted neurosurgeon, a former professor at Harvard University, past president of the American Holistic Medical Association, and the author of *Occult Medicine Can Save Your Life*,...[and] also works in conjunction with psychics and spiritists such as Caroline Myss. When Dr. Shealy was unable to help, he referred Carole to Dr. Robert Leichtman, MD, a spiritist who is coauthor of several dozen books received by revelation from "the spirits."

The Heart of Yoga Revealed

Leichtman admitted that Carole's situation was not uncommon among followers of Eastern gurus. He even told her some have died as a result of similar psychic attacks. But he too, was unable to help. His instructions, such as visualizing herself in the white "Christlight" of protection were useless. By this time, Carole was near the end: 'I had to endure the torture, unable to free myself. To those around me I was insane. No one believed me and no one could free me. The hopelessness I felt was unbearable. No one believed me except the psychics...and they could do nothing.

I was defenseless against these never-ending attacks...hundreds of presences filling my room, which itself would be filled with thick, ice cold air, my body drenched with perspiration as my whole body fought against them...

Filled with fear and exhaustion, on the brink of death, I screamed to my husband, 'I'm dying: I can't take it anymore. Get me to the hospital.'

[When Carole arrived at the hospital, frightened and] cowering on a cart the doctor on duty referred her to a psychiatrist whom she saw the next morning. 'He told me I was covering up some deep problems with the "talk of evil spirits. There is no such thing as the devil," he said coldly.... Upon returning home, the attacks

page 152

began again.... Although she was terrified of dying, death was now her desire.

But today, Carole is alive and well.... She is now in perfect health, both mentally and physically.

How did Carole get free? ... Carole attributes both her health and her life to a living Jesus Christ who delivered her from a desperate plight. Reflecting back on her predicament, she is awed that such terrible destruction could be purchased at the price of a simple, supposedly harmless form of yoga meditation. (*Encyclopedia of New Age Beliefs*, pg. 599-600)

Carole's story is not new, nor is she alone in suffering the effects of yoga possession. Elizabeth gives her testimony to confirm the truth of the evil of yoga and the power of God.

Elizabeth's testimony

Elizabeth was raised a Catholic, but when she was ex-communicated for being divorced, she thought that Jesus no longer wanted a relationship with her:

Being raised a Catholic, following my divorce from my abusive husband at the age of 19, the priest called me and told me I was excommunicated from the church. I always loved Jesus very much and probably had what one would call a "personal" relationship with Him as a young girl.

I was teaching religious education to the third graders in our parish church at the time of the divorce. Even the word "EX-COMMUNICATION" filled me with fear, loneliness, and despair. In my immature understanding of the dogma of the church, as opposed to the reality of Jesus' love, I was sure that Jesus no longer wanted to have "communion" with me.

As time went on without exercising my faith, I began using alcohol, drugs, imaging, meditation, and studying books on Eastern religion. Before I moved back home in 1970, I lived in California for 18 months. During that time, I had become a "hippy."

One day I found myself applying for work at a "Goodwill" store sorting rags at $1.65 /hr. so that I could bring home money to feed myself, my new "rock and roll" husband, and our commune.

More and more people were talking about yoga as a "natural high." People were becoming vegetarians and finding their own personal yogis. George Harrison had gone "eastern" and there were others who made it look good, healthy, and a viable alternative to the already alternative lifestyle I was living. I became a vegetarian and only used "natural" drugs like marijuana and began to limit my drinking alcohol. It was easy to learn Hatha Yoga. I felt more physically fit.

Classes were offered everywhere in my home town and available on TV.

A new center opened which taught Kundalini Yoga. My friends all agreed it would be beneficial to try a "further" kind of yoga to get the power I needed to control my life. A new class was starting, and I found myself in a room with others on a little rug in the meditation pose learning the breathing exercises to awaken the Kundalini power within.

Something entered my body

After about 10 minutes of doing the exercise, I screamed (not a cool thing to do in a yoga class) and shouted that something had come into me. I sensed it in my mind but could not identify it. It was alien, it was not me. I was extremely frightened.

The leaders took me out of the room onto the porch where they began massaging my feet (reflexology). I asked what had happened, and they said that this sometimes "happened" in their meetings without any explanation at all. They rubbed my feet until I calmed down. They wanted me off their porch as much as I wanted out of there. There was no concern shown for what had happened to me, and I left with more than I had ever bargained for.

I cannot say that this entity in me made me do things. It would whisper often, most of which I recognized as trash and lies. The one thing it was able to do was to torment me as it now lived somewhere inside of me. The worst thing for me was not being able to sleep. When I closed my eyes, especially at night but also at other times, I could see "it" manifest as a large red eye. I acknowledged that my behavior was becoming more erratic as I became more and more sleep-deprived. I often drank too much so that I could just pass out.

I began to despair of ever getting a regular night's sleep. My marriage was suffering as were friendships. Soon I became desperate and seeing no way out, I tried to take my own life. I remember being so angry when I woke up after what I was sure would be a sufficient drug overdose. I was admitted to the psychiatric ward at the University Hospital where I had been working as a lab technician since I had insurance there. I was given Thorazine which made my tongue and throat swell up and almost cut off respiration. I quickly calmed down on my own and got out of there.

I was admitted on two other occasions to hospitals and quickly learned the ropes in the "psych" business. No drugs were administered because of my suicide attempt and the allergic reaction to Thorazine. As long as I acted "appropriately," they thought they were helping me. I was alternately diagnosed with Bipolar Disorder, Schizophrenia, and whatever psychosis of the month they were currently studying. I quit my job while in the hospital. Now I had no work, no insurance, a husband who had washed his hands of me, and I eventually had to apply for welfare just to have a roof over my head. There is about a year and a half which is rather run together. A panel of five psychiatrists at the State Mental Hospital, where I finally found myself, listened to me explain my problem. I had a demon that lived in me, and I wanted to get rid of it. They had no answers to my plea.

I still had a problem with sleeping which bothered the night staff as they had to pay attention to where I was. One particular night I was in the dayroom by myself at 1:30 a.m., again upset because I couldn't sleep. My eyes fell on a big book which I recognized as a Bible. I thought why not pick it up and look at it? I opened the book to "Greater is He who is in you than he who is in the world." I didn't even know it had an address which I later found was I John 4:4.

The power of Jesus' name!

When I read those words a miracle happened, and Jesus showed me that although I had left Him, He had never left me. I was overjoyed and called on His Name, Jesus. I think I said it out loud, and when I did the demon left me. I knew it. I had peace, and for the first time in a long time I could get some sleep.

On my way to my room, four men who worked there grabbed me, each taking a limb and hauled me into solitary confinement. The nurse came and gave me a shot which I could tell was Thorazine. I spent the night screaming out the window to Jesus to save me yet again. He wouldn't have delivered me just to let me die from this drug they had administered. I felt the effects of the drug dissipating, another miracle.

Now I called out to the nurse that I smelled smoke. She told me to be quiet. But in fact, the woman who was in the solitary room next to mine had matches with her and started a fire with her bed clothes and mattress. I again prayed that Jesus would not let me die at this time but remembered what He said, "Greater is He who is in you than he who is in the world." I was content and made no more calls to the nurse.

Finally they too smelled and saw the smoke. The fire was put out, and by now it was morning. I was released that morning from the hospital. I never saw a doctor or understood how they knew I had been delivered. I began a long trip back, not knowing the pain I had caused or who I had hurt. I made amends the best I knew how.

My mother never stopped praying for me, and I am so grateful to her for that. The demon would try to come back to torment me, but I found that saying the Name of Jesus over and over again would make him go away. Finally, he quit trying. I guess he didn't want to hear that Name anymore. Eight months after I was released from the hospital, I met Lee. We were married 6 weeks after we met.

I once had fear from not being able to sleep but have learned to trust Jesus in that as well. My husband will bind the spirit of insomnia away from us many nights, and this attack from the spirit realm will stop. I knew Jesus as my Savior but now I know Him as my LORD. His Holy Spirit shows me the Way to live and move and have my being – His Name is Jesus.

Elizabeth and her husband of 34 years served the LORD in many varied ways. Over the years the LORD led them to minister in Haiti, Poland, and the Ukraine. While in Australia, they shared the Gospel of Jesus Christ and witnessed salvations resulting in the breakup of a cult numbering over one hundred people. Some of their other outreaches included the gathering and shipping of food and clothing to the former Soviet Union to aid the Jewish people. They also cared for the elderly, sick, and dying.

Elizabeth's personal testimony demonstrates God's love and ability to deliver us from any situation. All we have to do is call on Him in our time of trouble, and He will deliver us from the enemy (Psalm 41:1).

Elizabeth became ensnared by the lure of the promise of natural health, but found only danger. Christians aren't the only ones who are manipulated by the evil of yoga. The yoga masters themselves admit to its menacing power. Gopi Krishna, founder of one of many Kundalini research centers, testifies about his personal experience with Kundalini yoga:

> It was variable for many years, painful, obsessive, even fantasmic. I have passed through almost all the stages of different mediumistic, psychotic, and other types of mind; for some time I was hovering between sanity and insanity.
>
> I was writing in many languages, some of which I never knew [the occult ability of automatic writing]. (*Encyclopedia of New Age Beliefs*, pg. 608)

Gopi Krishna lists almost every form of mental disorder, from hardly noticeable aberrations to the most horrible forms of insanity, to neurotic and paranoid states, to megalomania (delusions of grandeur). He believes that most schizophrenics and manic depressives represent "malfunctioning" Kundalini energy.

Gopi Krishna, unarmed with the truth provided in God's Word, is left to reason in his mind using the enemy's lies. In his final summations regarding the devastating caustic yoga, Krishna concludes that the "malfunction" that comes from performing yoga is due to the fault of the human body to process the power of the aroused Kundalini. The body of the practitioner is either "not attuned to it with the help of various (yoga) disciplines or not genetically mature for it" (pg. 608).

Carole, Elizabeth, nor Krishna experienced a "malfunction of Kundalini energy." The Kundalini functioned perfectly according to its evil purpose. They all experienced an invasion of a demonic spirit.

Unfortunately, in spite of the admitted hazards of yoga, there are too many unsuspecting Christians practicing and subjecting themselves to its dangers. The person who experiences Kundalini's arousal will experience spiritual possession:

> A leading guru, Swami Muktananda, reveals that he was violently shaken by a spirit as part of the divine "work" of Kundalini within him. "A great deity in the form of my guru has spread all through me as chiti [energy] and was shaking me," and "when I sat for meditation my whole body shook violently, just as if I were possessed by a god or a bad spirit." (pg. 610)

Swami Muktananda explains the presence of the spirit working its yoking evil:

> "Simply by being in Yogi Desai's presence we had all experienced, to some degree, the awakening of the Shakti [power]. How this comes about is somewhat mysterious.... My body filled with a brilliant white light and I allowed myself to be absorbed in it." Yogi Desai explains that the astral body of the guru merges with that of the disciple.... The psychic energy is transferred directly from guru to disciple.... (pg. 610)

Then he describes the phenomenon of mass possession:

> There is also the phenomenon of mass possession
> which can occur among disciples gathered to hear
> the guru. This may end with the disciple finding
> himself in an involuntarily assumed position
> of worship of the guru, and, characteristically,
> worshiping the spirit entity possessing the guru:
> "When I opened my eyes again I noticed that
> my body had bent forward; my forehead was
> touching the floor. I do not remember assuming
> that position. I was actually bowing down to yogi
> Desai! I had never bowed to anyone in my life
> but some inner unknown force had prompted
> me.... [Yogi Desai] was surrounded by persons...
> on the floor around him, holding his feet, even
> kissing his feet." (pg. 610)

Swami Muktananda and the other attending gurus got
more than they bargained for. They were willing to yoke
with Brahman (the Universal World Soul), but instead they
were spiritually seduced into bowing down in worship to Yogi
Desai.

One Taoist yoga master observed that at some point in
your life of yoga practice, you will indeed experience demons
entering your body:

> The Taoist Master Chao Pi Ch'en observed that
> "as time passes, demonic states will occur to
> the [Kundalini yoga] practiser [sic]..." (592:18).
> Significantly, yogic energy manifestations and
> possession are sometimes initially sensed by the

experiencer as the work of an evil spirit. But this primary impression is "corrected" in accordance with Hindu theory, classifying the phenomena as a "divine process." (pg. 609)

What the Bible calls demonic possession, Hindu theory calls a divine process. You know the truth. You can clearly see that yoga is a demonic process, not divine. Yogis may not want to admit the truth, but even they know that the Kundalini serpent power projects its own will and its own agenda into the body of the yoga practitioner:

> ...I really felt frightened, as the power seemed something which could consume me.

> ...Your mind gets influenced spiritually as if some spirit has taken possession of your body and under that influence different postures of yoga are involuntarily performed without the pain or fatigue.

> ... It seemed that I was being controlled by some power which made me do all these things. I no longer had a will of my own. (pg. 610)

These occult occurances do not suggest that we are dealing with an impersonal energy. They suggest that we are dealing with demonic entities whose goal is spiritual deception and personal ownership.

Yoga is an insidious and extremely dangerous ritual. The Christian churches offering yoga classes are ignorant of yoga's roots and agenda and therefore cannot teach the truth of such occult practices. However, every enlightened Christian must know about the dark secrets of yoga.

In these last days we must educate ourselves with God's Word and follow Jesus Christ more closely, praying in the spirit because **prayers bring life**. We must hold tightly to the Word of God and stay alert to the leading of the Holy Spirit. Otherwise, Christians may find themselves entangled in yoga, seduced by its claims to offer physical health, spiritual power, and enlightenment. But in the end, yoga brings **poses that kill**.

Chapter 11

God's Miracles and Signs and Wonders

"Great and Marvelous are Your works, Lord God
Almighty! Just and true are Your ways O King
of the Saints!" (Revelation 15:3b, NKJ)

Throughout the Bible, God shows us His great and
marvelous works, His unlimited power to which
nothing can compare:

For who in the heavens can be compared to the
LORD? Who among the sons of the mighty can
be likened to the LORD? (Psalm 89:6, NKJ)

The heavens are Yours, the earth also is Yours;
The world and all its fullness, You have founded
them. (Psalm 89:11, NKJ)

Our loving Father God does great miracles through His
children. He shows us His healing powers and His creative
miracles. By His Holy Spirit, we know His love and His mercy.
We give Him all the praise and the glory. A picture of God's
mercy is revealed in the book of Exodus. The miracles God
performed through Moses' and Aaron's acts of faith were
done in order to bring the children of Israel out of bondage.
Because of their faith and His covenant, He is moved with
compassion when He hears the cries of His children:

God delivers us

Now it happened in the process of time that the
king of Egypt died. Then the children of Israel
groaned because of the bondage, and they cried
out; and their cry came up to God because of
the bondage. So God heard their groanings, and
God remembered His covenant with Abraham,
with Isaac, and with Jacob. (Exodus 2:23-24,
NKJ)

[And God told Moses] "So I will stretch out My
hand and strike Egypt with My wonders which I
will do in its midst; and after that he [Pharaoh]
will let you go." (Exodus 3:20, NKJ)

God then instructed Moses about how He would turn
Aaron's rod into a serpent so that Pharaoh would believe that
the LORD God had appeared to him (Exodus 4:5):

So Moses and Aaron went to Pharaoh, and they
did so, just as the LORD commanded. And Aaron
cast down his rod before Pharaoh and before his
servants, and it became a serpent. But Pharaoh
also called the wise men and the sorcerers; so the
magicians of Egypt, they also did in like manner
with their enchantments. For every man threw
down his rod, and they became serpents. But
Aaron's rod swallowed up their rods. (Exodus
7:10-12, NKJ)

In the days of Exodus the devil, through "wise men" and
sorcerers, imitated God's supernatural power. He still mimics

it to this day. He knows he can greatly influence mankind and lead them astray with the false mirroring of that power. In order for you to perform these imitative miracles, you must first be a willing vessel.

> "You are of your father the devil, and the desires
> of your father you want to do." (John 8:44a, NKJ)

Satan must find someone who is practicing occult rituals or committing any sin that affords him legal entry, because sin is the open door that gives place to the devil. Satan must use a person to facilitate these deceptive feats of magic.

In the book of Exodus, demonic powers are "given place" through the magicians of Egypt. They were practitioners of magic called "wise men" who mocked God by performing enchantments and sorceries as Pharaoh commanded.

God always prevails, even when Satan uses "wise men" and sorcerers to perform his enchantments. *Webster's New World Dictionary, Third College Edition* defines the word, "enchantment" as (1) to cast a spell over, as by magic; bewitch. Those who perform yoga use enchantments and magic in order to manifest exploits, which imitate God's miracles.

Satan's parlor tricks performed through mankind sorely pale in contrast to God's creative miracles of signs and wonders. Yogis claim that they can perform feats of death and resurrection through yogic practices of "Indian magic" and "secret preparations," and can remain in a "death trance for one hour."

By the power of the Holy Spirit, Jesus Christ (the Anointed One) demonstrated His resurrection power to bring life to the dead in John Chapter 11. He raised Lazarus from the grave after he had been dead for **four days**:

> [Jesus declared] "Lazarus, come forth!" And he who died came out bound hand and foot with graveclothes, and his face was wrapped with a cloth. Jesus said to them, "Loose him, and let him go." (John 11:43b, 44, NKJ)

If you don't bow to idols, you won't get burned!

In the third and fourth chapters of Daniel, God's miracles are revealed. His incredible power over the element of fire demonstrates to us His miraculous provision for those who do not bow to or serve other gods.

In the province of Babylon (current day Iraq) King Nebuchadnezzar set up an idol to be worshiped and it was announced among the people what was expected of them:

> "To you it is commanded, O peoples, nations, and languages, that at the time you hear the sound of the horn, flute, harp, lyre and psaltery, in symphony with all kinds of music, you shall fall down and worship the gold image that King Nebuchadnezzar has set up; and whoever does not fall down and worship shall be cast immediately into the midst of a burning fiery furnace." (Daniel 3:4-6, NKJ)

Verses eight through thirteen explain that after the symphony sounded, the "Chaldeans" came to Nebuchadnezzar. Chaldeans are astrologers, those who commit occult practices forbidden by God (Strong's Concordance, ref. 3778, pg 76). They came to Nebuchadnezzar with news of "heresy" in the land:

> "There are certain Jews whom you have set over the affairs of the province of Babylon; Shadrach, Meshach, and Abed-Nego; these men, O' King, have not paid due regard to you, they do not serve your gods or worship the gold image which you have set up." Then Nebuchadnezzar in rage and fury, gave the command to bring Shadrach, Meshach, and Abed-Nego... [and said] ..."if you do not worship, you shall be cast immediately into the midst of a burning fiery furnace. And who is the god who will deliver you from my hands?" (Daniel 3:12-15, NKJ)

The Jewish men replied:

> "If that is the case, our God whom we serve is able to deliver us from the burning fiery furnace, and He will deliver us from your hand, O king, but if not, let it be known to you, O king, that we do not serve your gods, nor will we worship the gold image which you have set up." (17-18)

Verse 19 says that because "Nebuchadnezzar was full of fury," he ordered the furnace to be heated, "seven times more than it was usually heated." He commanded them to be thrown into the burning fiery furnace.

Jesus is with us even in the fire!

Nebuchadnezzar was astonished and asked, "Did we not cast three men bound into the midst of the fire?" (24). His men responded with, "True, O King."

Nebuchadnezzar observes:

> "Look!" he answered, "I see four men loose, walking in the midst of the fire; and they are not hurt, and the form of the fourth is like the Son of God." (25)

> Then Shadrach, Meshach, and Abed-Nego came from the midst of the fire.... And they saw these men on whose bodies the fire had no power; and the hair of their head was not singed nor were their garments affected, and the smell of fire was not on them. (26b-27)

If God is for us, who can be against us? (Rom. 8:31)

> And we know that all things work together for good to those who love God, to those who are the called according to His purpose. For whom He foreknew, He also predestined to be conformed to the image of His Son, that He might be the firstborn among many brethren. Moreover, whom He predestined, these He also called; whom He called, these He also justified; and whom He justified, these He also glorified. (Romans 8:28-30, NKJ)

What a miracle! God's provision for those who do not bow and serve other gods is extraordinarily powerful. As we serve the Living God in word and deed, we too experience this covenant of provision and safety. As we know, when we sin against God and bow and serve other gods through any occult practice, we open ourselves to the sin of idol worship giving place to the devil:

> [Do not]...give place to the devil. (Ephesians 4:27)

> ...And have no fellowship with the unfruitful works of darkness, but rather expose them. (Ephesians 5:11)

> ...See then that you walk circumspectly, not as fools but as wise, redeeming the time, because the days are evil. (5:15-16, NKJ)

Many apostate churches, those who have abandoned faith in Jesus Christ, His power, and His Word are starving to the point of **atrophy**:

> n. a wasting away esp. of body tissue, an organ, etc. or the failure of an organ or part to grow or develop, as because of insufficient nutrition. (*Webster's New World Dictionary, Third College Dictionary*)

If these churches don't turn from starvation, and feed upon His Word, no one will look for salvation there. The body of Christ must feed upon His eternal Word, the "Bread of Life," to become fit.

"I am the bread of life. He who comes to Me
shall never hunger, and he who believes in Me
shall never thirst." (John 6:35, NKJ)

As we are made wise by Godly wisdom, we avoid the
pitfalls set before us by Satan, who "walks about like a roaring
lion, seeking whom he may devour" (I Peter 5:8). How do
we gain this marvelous Godly wisdom? According to James
1:5 and 6, we need only to ask God in faith. We are to know
God's Word, believe it, and act on it. God's Word is the
sustaining "bread of life," and Jesus is the "Living Bread:"

"I am the living bread which came down from
heaven. If anyone eats of this bread, he will live
forever; and the bread that I shall give is My
flesh, which I shall give for the life of the world."
(John 6:51, NKJ)

In the sixth chapter of John, Jesus demonstrated that He
is the Living Bread and the giver of life when he performed
a miracle and multiplied five loaves of bread and two small
fish to feed the masses. After giving thanks to the Father, He
fed five thousand men and countless women and children.
Amazingly, there was food left over, enough to fill twelve
baskets.

The LORD fought for Israel

A supernatural event recorded in Joshua 10:12-14 is
another example of God's covenant miracles. Joshua called
out to the LORD to cause the sun and the moon to stand
still until the people of God were triumphant in battling the
enemy:

So the sun stood still in the midst of heaven, and did not hasten to go down for about a whole day. (Joshua 10:13b, NKJ)

Joshua believed God. And behold, says the Scripture, the sun stood still that day. This cosmic occurrence has been substantiated in the scientific arena and is noted in an issue of *Christ for the Nations* magazine:

> The ancient Polynesians have a record in their traditions of a day when the normal hours were disrupted. However, instead of having additional daylight hours, they had additional hours of night.

> [...furthermore] Consider the tradition of the Maori of New Zealand. Their parallel account of Joshua's long day was that of a long night. Since Israel, where Joshua's battle occurred, is on the opposite side of the earth from New Zealand, this would be expected. (*Christ for the Nations*, magazine, Feb 2002, pg. 7)

God's Word brings salvation to the lost

We celebrate the absolute faithfulness of God's Word. "It shall not return to Me void, but it shall accomplish what I please, and it shall prosper in the thing for which I sent it" (Isaiah 55:11b). God's Word brings salvation to the lost. Eternal salvation is the greatest of all God's miracles: mankind re-united with his Creator.

This miracle of salvation restores sinful mankind to the Father by the perfect sinless blood sacrifice of the "Lamb of God," His only begotten Son:

> Blessed be the God and Father of our LORD Jesus Christ, who according to His abundant mercy has begotten us again to a living hope through the resurrection of Jesus Christ from the dead, to an inheritance incorruptible and undefiled and that does not fade away, reserved in heaven for you, who are kept by the power of God through faith for salvation ready to be revealed in the last time. (I Peter 1:3-5, NKJ)

Why does God perform these miracles? He wants to bring us into eternal union with Him. The new Heaven is described as being an eternal place where we dwell in the very presence of the Father and of the Lamb (Rev. 21:1):

> There shall no longer exist there anything that is accursed.... But the throne of God and of the Lamb shall be in it, and His servants shall worship Him.... They shall see His face, and His name shall be on their foreheads. And there shall be no more night; they have no need for lamp light or sunlight, for the LORD God will illuminate them and be their light, and they shall reign forever and ever. (Rev. 22:3-5, Amplified)

This eternal union is the fulfillment of God's Word for mankind. Our perfect destiny is to reign forever with our Creator. Heaven is God's glorious manifestation of His eternal plan:

Forever, O LORD, Your Word is settled in heaven.
(Psalm 119:89, NKJ)

"And behold, I am coming quickly, and My
reward is with Me, to give to everyone according
to his work. I am the Alpha and the Omega, the
Beginning and the End, the First and the Last."
(Rev. 22:12-13, NKJ)

God is our all in all. We have everything we need in
Christ Jesus. We don't need yoga's lying signs and wonders.
They are manifestations of the devil's temptations which are
meant to glorify mankind. God's miracles, signs, and wonders
are for His glory, and when Jesus is glorified, he will draw all
people to Himself (John 12:32).

Chapter 12

Union with the Spirit of Antichrist

> Little children, it is the last hour; and as you have heard that the Antichrist is coming, even now many antichrists have come, by which we know that it is the last hour. (I John 2:18, NKJ)

It should be no surprise to the children of God who study the Bible that we are approaching the end of the age. Jesus teaches that there will be distinctive indicators that mankind is approaching the Day of the LORD (Matt. 24:4-14).

These indicators are called the seven signs, the first of which is religious deception. Jesus said... "Take heed that no one deceives you. For many will come in My name, saying, 'I am the Christ,' and will deceive many" (Matt. 24:4-5).

Religious deception? In order to determine what is or is not religious we must seek the Word of God. We must be very careful about the use of the term "religious." Satan deceives through this misunderstanding of the word "religious." Throughout Scripture we are told to be aware of those "religious" persons, called false prophets, who come as "wolves in sheep's clothing" [claiming to be Christ] (Matt. 7:15).

Lucifer, the original "wolf in sheep's clothing," initiated a worshipful practice of sign language gestures, prayer positions, and bowing, which is done in a religious and reverent manner. Yoga rituals contain devotional bowing postures as part of their choreographed religious routine which deceives many into believing they are worshiping Christ through yoga.

According to one demonology specialist, religiosity is a ploy used by Satan:

> The devil does not want to take away our religiousness; his real desire is to sever us from Christ and to prevent us from following him. (*A Manual for Demonology and the Occult*, Kent Philpott, pg. 144)

The Antichrist is mounting an offense for the battle of the "end times." Through yoga's religious discipline, he is increasing his demonic communication with mankind. A compelling fascination and openness for the supernatural, without regard to God's Word, has afforded Satan a perfect opportunity to introduce many into the occult:

> Occult practices encourage and often demand openness to spirits.... The occult medium is purposely trained to enter into passive or altered states of mind so that a trance state (an openness to spirits) might be achieved...Most occultists believe they are in contact with good or neutral spirits, not suspecting that these spirits are demons. Much Satan worship in the occult, then is in disguise. Instead of placating or using

spirits or spirit guides, occultists are actually trafficking with demons. (pg. 91)

Many Americans, confused about the terms "religion, spirituality, and supernatural," are easily deceived into believing that an encounter with any of these terms is a meeting with God Almighty. This unfortunate confusion brings millions of Christians to their yoga mats in an attempt to become more "spiritual." The Antichrist spirit, not the Holy Spirit, is encountered on the yoga mat. By trafficking with demons, the yoga practitioner has glorified Satan, not God.

Yoga could very well be the catalyst, which ushers in the Antichrist's reign. This phenomenal movement, spreading rapidly, continues to explode as the occult religions of the world unite in one spiritual union with the Universal World Soul. Widespread effects will be devastating. We will begin to witness an increase in psychic phenomenon and displays of satanic physical power.

One critical expression of Satan's power is to keep mankind from the truth by twisting biblical prophecy. He distorts the prophecy of the second coming of Christ by confusing people into worshiping the Antichrist (1 John 2:22, 4:3, 2 John 7).

The LORD will appear from Heaven

Bible believing Christians know Jesus Christ, the Messiah, will not return to the earth through the womb of a woman and grow into manhood as in His first coming. This truth is clearly stated in Matthew:

> ...if anyone says to you, 'Look, here is the Christ!' or 'There!' do not believe it. (Matt. 24:23, NKJ)

> For as the lightning comes from the east and flashes to the west, so also will the coming of the Son of Man be (vs. 27). Then the sign of the Son of Man will appear in heaven, and then all the tribes of the earth will mourn, and they will see the Son of Man coming on the clouds of heaven with power and great glory. (Matt 24:30, NKJ)

Unfortunately, even sects within the Jewish communities have been following deceiving spirits that are part of the Antichrist kingdom. One such false religion's philosophy is called Kabbalah. Kabbalah is found in *Webster's New World Dictionary, Third College Edition*, referenced by its root name, "Cabala. Cabala means (1.) an occult philosophy of certain Jewish rabbis, esp. in the Middle Ages, based on a mystical interpretation of the Scriptures, and (2.) any esoteric or secret doctrine; occultism."

Rebekah Kenton reveals a Kabbalistic view of the chakras. "The awakening of any chakra is rarely a sudden event. It may take several years or lifetimes." Note how Kabbalah embraces the lie of the eastern mystic belief in reincarnation. Furthermore, Kenton claims that "In Kabbalah, an individual whose [seven] chakras have fully and permanently awakened would be called the Messiah" (www.adishakty.org/miscellaneous/battle_of_armageddon.htm. pg. 5,8).

These enlightened yogis calling themselves "Messiahs" believe they are the salvation for themselves and many others.

Yoga permits us to experience our own self-salvation through the self-realization that no more resurrections will be necessary. We have arrived as our own Messiah!

The mark of the beast

Many antichrist spirits are jockeying for position as the end-time "Messiah." False prophets and antichrists who have come on the world scene believe that through yoga they can obtain god-hood. False messiahs are being reported from time to time. Research reveals as early as 1909, a Hindu named Krishnamurti, a forerunner for the "mark of the beast," (Rev. 13:18) desired to bear the number of the Antichrist's name, 666:

> [He] is a disciple of Theosophy and a Hindu. In 1909 Annie Besant, then head of the Theosophical Society headquartered in India, announced that through Yoga and meditation it had been revealed to her that the young Krishnamurti had been chosen to be the "World Teacher and Guiding Spirit of the Universe." Besant prophesied that the "Christ" spirit – he who directs the invisible hierarchy – would manifest itself by taking possession of Krishnamurti's body. (*Dark Secrets of the New Age,* by Texe Marrs, pg 250)

Many eastern mystic believers attested to the fact that Krishnamurti was to be the long-awaited "Christ" as they listened to him speak "in the first person as god." According to this report, nearly six thousand delegates were there, and "some knelt down and worshiped Krishnamurti." There were others who witnessed "a great coronet of brilliant, shimmering blue appearing above his head.... Besant, ... predicted that the new 'Messiah' would combine all religions into one. Then he would create a world government" (pg. 251).

Leaving Europe by boat for America, Krishnamurti docked in New York City. Upon arrival he "complained about the electrical atmosphere." He said that he was "unable to meditate successfully" and his "spirit guide mentors were unable to function." The young Hindu became "incoherent" aboard ship during an interview, according to The New York Times. His further speaking engagements were canceled and "he sailed back to his native India a failure" (pg. 251).

Since then, there have been several others like Krishnamurti. According to the Tare Center, Lord Maitreya, avatar and world teacher, is the one Christians call Christ, whom the Jews term Messiah, the Buddhists call the Fifth Buddha, and the Hindus call Krishna. These are all names for one individual (pg. 251).

Claiming to be Christ doesn't make one Christ. Satan is a counterfeiter. He established counterfeit religions. These counterfeit religions claim to have open arms for all religions but blatantly have zero tolerance for the Bible, the Ten Commandments, prayer in our schools and stadiums, the Nativity Scene, and our national motto, "In God we trust." In other words, a counterfeit religion abhors Christianity.

The Antichrist spirit has permeated western "religious" thinking to the point that many members in American churches are deserters of the faith. These are apostate members who are rebels and renegade adversaries, denying the truth of Jesus Christ.

Yoga union with Kundalini - a "living religion?"

This zero tolerance for Christianity is evident in Sahaja yoga. According to a Sahaja yoga devotee, Christianity is "dead, just nonsense…, another foolish, stupid religion which has no meaning." This devotee, obviously in union with the spirit of antichrist, advises us to look to the Indian Sahaja yogi for a living religion which brings union with Kundalini, the Universal Unconscious (www.adishakti.org/miscellaneous/Battle_of_Armageddon.htm pg. 14).

> Sahaja yoga is a living religion which convinces you through the living proof of the Kundalini's manifestation. When it is properly established in a realized soul the subject can decode without difficulty the different sensations within the fingers, spine and brain. He reads the Universal Unconscious. (Gregoire de Kalbermatten, The Advent, The Life Eternal Trust Publishers 1979, pgs. 165-66 from www.adishakti.org pg. 17)

Burning vibrations act as a correcting instrument

According to this same website, if the yoga practitioner thinks "wrongly [contrary to Sahaja yoga], the vibratory awareness" reacts as a "correcting instrument" within the practitioner's chakras. There is "a sensation of burning" which occurs as a reaction to the awakened deities (pg. 17).

Any resistance to the Kundalini is suddenly experienced because the Hindu deities are alive within the yogis realized soul. According to Sahaja yoga devotees, this reaction to "wrong thinking... drastically reduces the chances of a realized soul making a mistake" (www.adishakti.org pgs. 16, 17). The term "mistake" means any thinking contrary to the religion of Sahaja yoga.

The yoga master Shri Mataji Nirmala Devi claims that the Kundalini is equal to Jesus Christ and the Holy Spirit. The Kundalini makes us "born-again" and "baptizes" us into new life:

> [T]he Kundalini has the power to bring forth the complete nourishment and adjustment of the disturbed genes. When She is awakened, She changes the series of genes. Not only that She corrects the gene's data base but She breaks through the fontanel bone area and connects the seeker to all the pervading power of Divine Love also called the cool breeze of the Holy Ghost, Ruh Pitambhora or Parama Chaitanya. Thus one, by this second birth, becomes a realized person as actualization of Baptism takes place..... It is a resurrection process, like an egg becoming the bird...The genes change and complete transformation takes place. [The yogi] respects all the religions and belongs to a Universal religion which encompasses all the religions of the world... [A]ging does not take place, on the contrary, the Sahaja yogi becomes and looks at least 20 years younger than his age.

They become universal beings... [A] new race of saints are created. (Message of Metascience as quoted in www.adishakti.org, pgs. 11, 12)

Certainly this is not how the Bible describes being born again (John 3:3-17), nor does this occult manifestation of the Kundalini describe the baptism of the Holy Spirit (Acts 1:4-8). And certainly the results of being born again into the Kingdom of God by the Holy Spirit would not bring us into union with "all of the religions of this world."

In fact, as born again Christians, we are to be separate from the world (John 17:9-18). Those who practice the lawless Antichrist religions of the world are deceived. The Bible warns us of the serpent's craftiness, denying the true Christ, preaching a different gospel and a different spirit:

> For I [Paul] am jealous for you with the jealousy of God Himself. I promised you as a pure bride to one husband – Christ. But I fear that somehow your pure and undivided devotion to Christ will be corrupted, just as Eve was deceived by the cunning ways of the serpent. You happily put up with whatever anyone tells you, even if they preach a different Jesus than the one we preach, or a different kind of Spirit than the one you received, or a different kind of gospel than the one you believed. (II Corinthians 11:2-4 New Living Translation)

Kundalini's connection to the spirit of the Antichrist aggressively encourages people to receive the "power of the serpent. The "christ" of the yogic realization is "Kundalini," the serpent of Antichrist, not the LORD Jesus Christ.

The Kundalini "christ" attempts to usher in Satan's prideful "Last Days" agenda, which includes the notion that Kundalini has equality with Jesus. In his lust for power, Kundalini claims to be the "**mediator**" between man and God.

Satan, through his Antichrist spirit of the serpent "Kundalini," positions himself as mediator between heaven and earth fulfilling his desire to be worshiped as God. Satan is attempting to usurp the position of Jesus Christ who is the only mediator between heaven and earth:

> For there is one God and one Mediator between God and men, the Man Christ Jesus, who gave Himself a ransom for all. (I Tim. 2:5,6a, NKJ)

> And for this reason He is the Mediator of the new covenant, by means of death, for the redemption of the transgressions under the first covenant, that those who are called may receive the promise of the eternal inheritance. (Heb. 9:15, NKJ)

Eternal inheritance is union with God in heaven and comes by receiving salvation through the blood of Jesus Christ. But according to New Age swamis, a spontaneous transformation of mankind in union with the "Universal World Soul" will come by way of Kundalini through yoga!

These yogis further prophesy that the New World Order and One World Religion will be led by one unparalleled [yoga] master who is incarnate. This yogi would be a master of the Kundalini and would teach all the people the ancient secrets of self-transformation (www.freedomofmind.com/groups/sahaja/second.html pg.12).

> ...the Kundalini would be awakened spontaneously through Sahaja yoga, that is, spontaneous union with the Divine, and become the means to both individual and collective transformation on a mass scale. (pg. 12)

Bhrigumuni, called "the first great astrologer" predicted in his book, *Nadi Granth*, that it is yoga that will usher in the end time event that he describes all religions are looking for:

> These are the times described in the Holy Bible as 'Last Judgment' and in the Koran as 'Klyama', the Resurrection Time. Astrologically, it is also called the Age of Aquarius, the time of rebirth and a great spiritual development on the earth. (pg. 12)

Yoga generates a mystical arousal for the occult, a stirring within the practitioner for empowerment and a dark desire for supernatural power. This unnatural desire to conquer the physical realm using psychic powers is common among the yoga masters.

In conquering the physical realm, yogis perform signs and lying wonders and supernatural feats of strength. These feats include levitation, simulated death and resurrection, self-generated heat, psychic surgery and healing, all of which are credited to the "spiritual" forces of the so-called mediator between God and man – the Kundalini serpent, an incredibly seductive spirit of Antichrist.

Kundalini sets herself up as God

Certainly the Kundalini fulfills the desires of the "man of sin, ... who opposes and exalts himself above all that is called God or that is worshiped, so that he sits as God in the temple of God, showing himself that he is God" (II Thessalonians 2:3b-4). We must be able to recognize yoga's obsessive compulsion for power. In their quest for power yoga adepts aspire to manipulate the natural physical laws of nature.

Even the satanic bible acknowledges that *power* is a goal of the occult. "Anton LaVey, head of San Francisco's Satanic Church, wrote in his *Satanic Bible*, 'No one ever pursued occult studies... without ego gratification and personal power as a goal'" (*A Manual of Demonology and the Occult*, pg. 88).

Satan wants to possess the flesh of humans and rule as God in order to further his evil kingdom on earth without the Body of Christ restraining him. The Antichrist spirit is using yoga to covertly accomplish demonic infiltration and possession of mankind.

Because of the work of Christ on the cross, Christians have authority through the power of the Holy Spirit to "cast out demons" (Matthew 10:1). Jesus says in Mark 16:17, "And these signs will follow those who believe: In My name they will cast out demons." Let us rebuke the Antichrist spirit and worship Almighty God in fear and reverence:

> The reverent and worshipful fear of the Lord
> is the beginning (the chief and choice part) of
> Wisdom, and the knowledge of the Holy One is
> insight and understanding. For by me [Wisdom
> from God] your days shall be multiplied, and the
> years of your life shall be increased.
> (Proverbs 9:10-11, Amplified)

We must not trade the wisdom of God for acclaimed power offered by the Antichrist spirit through yoga. We must not substitute knowledge of the Word for knowledge of the world.

As children of the Most High God, we are called out of darkness to stand against the spirit of Antichrist:

> You are a chosen generation, a royal priesthood,
> a holy nation, His own special people, that you
> may proclaim the praises of Him who called
> you out of darkness into His marvelous light.
> (I Peter 2:9, NKJ)

The Indian Language of Sanskrit

Acharya religious teacher

Agni the god of fire – engendering body heat, "tumo"

Aham Brahma Asmi I am Brahma, 1of 3 in the Hindu godhead

Ahamkara the "I" – sense

Ajana chakra brow (Siva, a Hindu god) centre, one of the seven energy centers in the body

Anahata chakra Heart (Siva, a Hindu god) centre, one of the seven energy centers in the body

Antaranga the three internal practices of meditation

Anusvara an extended nasalized sound of the sandskrit alphabet; an unpronounceable vibration capable of articulation in conjunction with the letter of the alphabet

Arcanā deity worship

Asamprajnata Samadhi unconscious Samadhi – the highest stage of yoga meditation; Self – Realization, Absorption

Asmita the sense of I-Am-ness

Asramas stages of life for the Hindu

Asura a demon

Atman the Self

AUM English translation for OM – sacred syllable or mantra representing the Absolute; I AM – god

Avatar earthly incarnation of a divinity

Bhagavad-Gita Hindu Holy Book

Bhakti pure devotional service to Lord Krisna

Bija, Bindu seed, point; semen seed

Brahma 1st god of the Hindu trinity – worship/prayer (the chief member of Hindu trinity with Vishnu & Siva)

Brahman the Higher-Self, the Absolute; the One; Ultimate Reality; Universal Spirit/Soul, the all-pervading impersonal aspect of Krsna

Buddhi intellect; wisdom

Buddhi Yoga Yoga of wisdom

Chakra an energy (Siva, a Hindu god) centre in the subtle body; totaling seven, meaning wheel

Chi universal energy – breath

Charkrasana "wheel" yoga posture

Cit pure consciousness

Darshama vision

Deva-Dasi temple prostitute – goddess

Dharana concentration; holding the attention steadily on an object – occult meditation

Dharma way of life; national consciousness of India

Dhyana contemplation; the free-flowing continuation of Dharana

Dhyana Yoga yoga of meditation or deep concentration – achieved through breathing techniques which aims to bring "enlightenment"

Drashta-Ordrashtri the Seer, Witness or Looker, esoteric – Hidden mysteries

Ganges a sacred river that flows from the lotus feet of Lord Visnu

Gāyatri a transcendental vibration chanted by brāhmanas

Gnosticism an occult salvation system, a system of unorthodox religious beliefs, an esoteric worldly view

Gunas the three inherent qualities of nature, (1) motion, (2) illumination, (3) durability

Hatha Yoga union with breath of the Atman (self) with the Higher-Self (universal world soul Brahman)

Isvara or Ishvara supreme cosmic soul; god, Brahman

Japa Repetitions of a mantra

Jnana Yoga yoga of Higher self-knowledge, union with universal world soul

Krishna black, dark, incarnation of Vishnu (Avatar) (2nd God of Hindu Trinity)

Kundalini (serpent power) activated during yoga to bring the practitioner "enlightenment" uniting man with "the universal world soul"

Lotus basic esoteric, cross-legged posture of yoga, a flower worshiped by Eastern mystics, also called, "Buddha Posture"

Lotus petals located on each of the seven chakras. The number of petals indicates the chakra's vibration frequency.

Maithuna sacramental coitus, (sexual intercourse) or spiritual union

Manas mind

Manipura chakra (Siva, a Hindu god) centre located in energy center of the solar plexus

Mantra power word, a sacred sound-symbol; incantation

Maya illusion, the illusory world

Mudra another word for posture, usually indicating hand gestures

Muladhara chakra (Siva, a Hindu god) centre – energy center located at the tail bone or root centre

Nad motion vibration

Nada internal sound

Nadi a channel of the subtle body through which Prana (life) flows; there are 72,000 nadis in the body

Nirvicard a grade of self-realization, absorption; "Nirvitarka" same (highest state of yoga) samadha

Ojas concentrated psychic power

OM I AM, god, also (sound recited to contact Isvara - Hindu god)

Padmasana lotus posture – represents the Hindu trinity
     ***Ardha-padmasana** half-lotus posture

Prana cosmic energy; life force; "breath of life"

Prana-Kriya, breath ritual (sacrifice of one's breath into the Divine)

Pranayama breath control used to achieve psychosomatic health and transpersonal state of dhyana

Raja Yoga yoga union of mental mastery with the "Universal World Soul"

Rajas one of three gunas; activity; energy; the kinetic (motion) principle

Sādhānā spiritual discipline

Sahasrara chakra (Siva) centre – energy center located at the crown of the head

Samadhi the highest stage of yoga meditation; self realization; absorption

Samskaras mental impressions

Sankirtana congregational chanting of the Lord's [Krisna] glories

Sariātana-dharma the eternal religion of the living being, to render service to the supreme Lord [Krisna]

Sattva the finest of the three gunas, purity, intelligence, and illumination

Savicara a grade of Samadhi

Savitarka a grade of Samadhi

Shakti goddess of creative powers – earth power – counterpart to Siva

Siva 2nd god of the Hindu trinity, dwells within 7 chakras of the subtle body, when united with Shakti brings "enlightenment" to the yogi

Siddha a sage, seer or perfected person

Siddhasana perfect posture

Siddhi psychic attainment or special power; example: telepathy

Srāmī one who can control his mind and senses

Sukghma Shavira the astral body

Sushumna central channel carrying Kundalini energy

Sutra thread; highly condensed, aphoristic method of literary expression – unconnected ideas behind Sanskrit words, precepts of Hinduism and Buddhism

Swadhisthana chakra (Siva, a Hindu god) energy centers located in the pelvic centre representing the Hindu god Siva

Tat tuam asi "That thou art"

Third-eye believed to be the place between the eyes on the forehead and also to be the portal for the enlightenment and ultimate wisdom

Tumo a psychic power engendering body heat in the body, Agni – the god of fire

Trataka gazing steadily at an object; one of the six purifying processes of Hatha Yoga.

Upanishads Hindu holy scriptures, mystical Hindu or Buddhist religious writings, 108 philosophical portions of the Vedas

Vedas section of Bhavagad-Gita

Vibhuti the Sanskrit word for divine power

Vishnu 3rd god of the Hindu trinity

Vishudda chakra (Siva, a Hindu god) energy center located in the throat centre

Yoga Hindu discipline meaning "union" with the divine or linking with the "Supreme" or union with the "Universal World Soul"

Zen Living Buddhism

Bibliography

Books/Magazines/Pamphlets/Newspapers/Internet

The Devil's Alphabet Kregel Publications, Grand Rapids, Michigan 49501, Library of Congress Catalogue, card no. 76-160692 ISBN 0-8254-30046 copyright 1972 (second printing)

The Little Book of Hindu deities, From the Goddess of Wealth to the Sacred Cow, by Sanjay Patel, Published by Penguin Group, 375 Hudson Street, NY, NY 10014, USA Copyright © 2006

Be a Frog, a Bird, or a Tree Rachel Carr's Creative Yoga Exercises for Children Prebound Library of Congress Copyright © 1973 by Rachel Carr, Harper Collins Publisher

The Heart of Yoga by T.K.V. Desikachar, Inner Traditions, Rochester, VT ©1995 T.K.V. Desikachar www.Innertraditions.com

Living Yoga Edited by George Feuerstein and Stephan Bodian editors, Copyright © 1993 by Yoga Journal. Used by permission of Jeremy P. Tarcher, and imprint of Penguin Group.

The Complete Yoga Book by James Hewitt Published by Rider, an imprint of Random Century Grout Ltd. In 1987, Reprinted 1987 and 1990. This edition published by Cresset Press an imprint of Random Century Group Ltd 20 Vauxhall Bridge Rd. London SWIV 25A

Bhagavad-Gita As It Is, text courtesy of The Bhaktivedanta Book Trust International, Inc. www.krishna.com. Used with permission.

Tal Brooke, *One World*, End Run Publishing, 1442A Walnut St., #387, Berkeley, CA 94709, copyright © 1989 and 2000. Used by permission.

Encyclopedia of New Age Beliefs, Copyright © 1996 by Harvest House Publishers, Eugene, Oregon 97402 Used by permission.

Like Lambs to the Slaughter by Johanna Michaelson, Harvest House Publisher, Eugene, Oregon 97402 Copyright ©1989 by Johanna Michaelson, Used by permission.

Dark Secrets of the New Age by Texe Marrs, Copyright ©1987 Crossway Book. Wheaton, Ill. A division of Good News Publications, 130 Crescent St., Wheaton, Ill. 60187

Confronting the New Age by Douglas Groothuis, forward by Walter Martin, Inter Varsity Press, Downers Grove, Ill. 60515 ©1988 by Douglas Groothuis

A Manual of Demonology and the Occult Kent Philpott, Zondervan Publishing House of the Zondervan Corporation/ Grand Rapids, Michigan 49506 copyright 1973

Mudras: Yoga in Your Hands by Gertrud Hirschi, Red Wheel/ Weiser Books, used with permission of Red Wheel/Weiser LLC, Newbury Port, Me and San Fransisco, Ca, www. redwheel/weiser.com, copyright © 2000, 800-423-7087

Kundalini: The Arousal of the Inner Energy, by Ajit Mookerjee, Destiny Books, Rochester, VT © 1986, Thames and Hudson

Ltd. London © 1982 www.InnerTraditions.com
Zen Around the World, A 2500 – year Journey from the Buddha to You, by Annellen M. Simpkins, C. Alexander Simpkins, Charles E. Tuttle Co. Inc. Boston • Rutland, Vermont • Tokyo, Copyright © 1997

Total Yoga – A Step-by-Step Guide to Yoga at Home for Everyone, by Tara Fraser, Duncan Baird Publishers, London, Sterling Publishing Co. Inc. 387 Park Ave. South New York, 10016 – 8810

The Shambhala Encyclopedia of Yoga by Georg Feuerstein, PHD, Shambhala Publications, Inc., Horticultural Hall 300 Massachusetts Ave. Boston, Mass. 02115 ©1997 by Georg Feuerstein

Martial Arts of the Orient by Peter Lewis, this edition published in the United Kingdom 1993 by MMB, an imprint of Multimedia Books Limited, 32-34 Gordon House Rd., London NW51LP

Strong's Exhaustive Concordance of the Bible James Strong, S.T.D., LLD World Bible Publishers, Inc. Copyright 1890, by James Strong, Madison, N.J. Copyright © 1980, 1986 assigned to World Bible Publishers, Inc.

Random House Websters College Dictionary, Copyright © 1992, 1991 by Random House, 201 E. 50th St., NY, NY 10022

Webster's New World Dictionary Third College edition of American English Victoria Neufeldt, Editor-in-chief David B. Guralnik, Emeritus Prentice Hall New York, NY Copyright © 1991, 1988 by Simon & Schuster, Inc.

Webster's Family Encyclopedia, Copyright © 1981 Laurence Urdang Associates, Ltd., Aylesbury, Copyright © 1985, 1987, 1989, 1991 Ottenheimer Publishers, Inc.

Encarta World English Dictionary, St. Martin's Press, 175 Fifth Ave., New York, NY 10010

New King James Version Holy Bible reader's edition Thomas Nelson Publishers, Nashville copyright © 1990 by Thomas Nelson, Inc.

New Living Translation, copyright © 1996. Tyndale House Publishing, Inc. Wheaton, Ill. 60189.

Amplified Bible, copyright © 1987 by the Zondervan Corporation and the Lockman Foundation, La Habra, Ca. 90631.

Comparing Christianity with the Cults, compiled by Keith L. Brooks, Irvine Robertson, and Dillon Burroughs, copyright 1969, 1975, 1976, 1985, 2007 by Moody Bible Institute.

Comparing Christianity with World Religions, compiled by Steven Cory and Dillon Burroughs, copyright 1969, 1975, 1976, 1985, 2007 by Moody Bible Institute.

Christ for the Nations magazine, Feb 2002 Issue, pg, 7 "Creation Science" with President Dennis Lindsay.

Jessie Milligan, Fort Worth Star Telegram "Yoga for the Mind," Mon., Oct.21, 2002

Terry Lee Goodrich, "Spiritual Stretch," Fort Worth Star

Telegram, May 5, 2007, 8B &9B

Mike Roizen and Mehment Oz, "You Docs," "Manipulations of the Breath" Fort Worth Star Telegram March 30, 2009, pg. 8A

The Honolulu Advertiser Tribune Media Services 10-03, "Letters and Commentary" Tuesday, October 21, 2003, A7,

Temple Daily Telegram, "Houston Judge Orders Man to Take Yoga Classes," Friday, Jan. 23, 2004

Kristen Holland, "Yoga Compliments Faith, Some Christians Say," Dallas Morning News, Sat. Aug. 9, 2003, 3G

Television Programs

The Wisdom Channel, "Pillars of Health," Sept. 16, 2004

ABC's "Prime Time Live" February 10, 2005, "John of God"

Internet

www.equip.org/free/CP0213.num (Christianity and Eastern Religions, CRI Perspective)

www.hinduwebsite.com/vedicdeities.htm (symbolism in Hinduism, the secret of the vedic gods)

www.adishakti.org/miscellaneous/battle_of_armageddon. htm (Prophecies of Nostradamus)

www.courses.rochesteredu/muller-ortega (Ganesha: our

research, presentation, and thoughts)
www.sahajayoga.org/QuotesAndTalks/Beijing.html (Shri Matajis talk on the global problems facing women today. Shri Matajis talk at UN Women's conference address by Dr. (Mrs.) Nirmala Srivastava to the Inter-Regional Round Table fourth World Conference on Women, Beijing, September 13, 1995

www.freedomofmind.com/groups/sahaja/second.htm (Freedom of Mind resource Steve Hassan Bookstore. Shri Mataji Nirmala Devi's Sahaja Yoga Second Coming? Or Mother of the Cults?

www.yogajournal.com/advertise/pressrelease/10

www.yogajournal.com/basics/822 (Yoga Beginners Expert Q&A – the meaning of "Namaste")

www.childrensyoga.com (children's yoga teacher sharing page 1-3 By Shakta Kaur Khalser)

www.onyoga.com/crisis/crisis.htm (Children's Yoga: Helping Children Cope With Crisis pg 1-4)

www.sunandmoonstudio.com/whole.html

www.letusreason.org

www.absw.org.uk/briefings/nitric%20oxide.htm

www.brainmysteries.com

www.rapidnet.com/jbeard/bdm/psychology/yoga.htm

About the Author

Judy White's personal deliverance out of the New Age movement was the catalyst to this book. As a spirit-filled evangelical Christian, she has addressed several venues including conferences, association meetings, and media interviews. She was privileged to be a guest on a PBS program aired in San Antonio, Texas while serving as chapter president of Aglow International.

The purpose of this book is to make the truth available to as many Christians as possible which includes pastors and churches, ministries and associations, hospital and school administrators and generally where ever yoga is taught or promoted.

Order Form

The Heart of Yoga Revealed!

To Order Online:

www.TheHeartof YogaRevealed.com

Or Write To:

Truth Cross Publishing, LLC.
PO Box 1488
Kingsland, Tx 78639

☐ Please send me _____ copy(s)
Enclosed is my payment of $ _____ (14.95 ea)
Plus Shipping $ _____ (3.00 ea)

Please make checks payable to
Truth Cross Publishing LLC

☐ Please charge my:

☐Master Card ☐Visa ☐Am. Express ☐Discover

Account #: _____

Exp. Date: _____ Security Code: _____

_____
Cardholder Signature

Send us Your
Comments/Testimonies

<u>The Heart of Yoga Revealed!</u>

_____

_____

_____

_____

_____

_____

_____

_____

_____

_____

_____

_____

_____

Truth Cross Publishing, LLC.
PO Box 1488
Kingsland, Tx 78639